CHRISTOPHER COLUMBUS
and the Age of Exploration
in World History

Titles *in World History*

**Captain Cook Explores
the Pacific
in World History**
0-7660-1823-7

**Christopher Columbus
and the
Age of Exploration
in World History**
0-7660-1820-2

**Cinqué of the *Amistad*
and the Slave Trade
in World History**
0-7660-1460-6

**Commodore Perry
Opens Japan to Trade
in World History**
0-7660-1462-2

**Cortés and the Conquest
of the Aztec Empire in
World History**
0-7660-1395-2

**Hernando de Soto
and the Spanish
Search for Gold
in World History**
0-7660-1821-0

**Julius Caesar and
Ancient Rome
in World History**
0-7660-1461-4

**King Henry VIII
and the Reformation
in World History**
0-7660-1615-3

**King Richard
the Lionhearted
and the Crusades
in World History**
0-7660-1459-2

**Lenin and the
Russian Revolution
in World History**
0-7660-1464-9

**Leonardo da Vinci and
the Renaissance
in World History**
0-7660-1401-0

**Mahatma Gandhi and
India's Independence
in World History**
0-7660-1398-7

**Nelson Mandela and
Apartheid in
World History**
0-7660-1463-0

**Philip II and Alexander
the Great Unify Greece
in World History**
0-7660-1399-5

**Pizarro and the
Conquest of the Incan
Empire in World History**
0-7660-1396-0

**Robespierre and the
French Revolution
in World History**
0-7660-1397-9

**Stanley and Livingstone
and the Exploration of
Africa in World History**
0-7660-1400-2

CHRISTOPHER COLUMBUS
and the Age of Exploration
in World History

Al Sundel

Enslow Publishers, Inc.

40 Industrial Road
Box 398
Berkeley Heights, NJ 07922
USA

PO Box 38
Aldershot
Hants GU12 6BP
UK

http://www.enslow.com

Library of Congress Cataloging-in-Publication Data

Sundel, Al.
 Christopher Columbus and the age of exploration in world history / Al
Sundel.
  p. cm.— (In world history)
 Includes bibliographical references and index:
 ISBN 0-7660-1820-2
 1. Columbus, Christopher—Juvenile literature. 2. Explorers—
America—Biography—Juvenile literature. 3. Explorers—Spain—
Biography—Juvenile literature. 4. America—Discovery and exploration—
Spanish—Juvenile literature. [1. Columbus, Christopher. 2. Explorers.
3. America—Discovery and exploration—Spanish.] I. Title. II. Series.
E111 .S9 2002
970.01'5'092—dc21
                                    2001002893

Printed in the United States of America

10 9 8 7 6 5 4 3 2 1

To Our Readers: We have done our best to make sure all Internet addresses in this
book were active and appropriate when we went to press. However, the author
and the publisher have no control over and assume no liability for the material
available on those Internet sites or on other Web sites they may link to. Any
comments or suggestions can be sent by e-mail to comments@enslow.com or to
the address on the back cover.

Illustration Credits: Al Sundel (Adapted from *Time* magazine), p. 61; Al
Sundel, pp. 15, 25, 26, 27, 30, 62, 90, 96, 109; American Museum of
Natural History, p. 103; British Museum, p. 33; Enslow Publishers, Inc.,
pp. 50, 56, 63, 83, 105; Library of Congress, pp. 6, 8, 20, 40, 44, 73, 79, 86,
93, 107, 112; © The Mariners' Museum, Newport News, Virginia, pp. 11,
47; National Archives, p. 17.

Cover Illustration: Enslow Publishers, Inc., (Background Map) and
Library of Congress (Columbus Portrait).

Contents

Christopher Columbus sailed into the unknown and discovered half the planet. There are only imagined portraits of him.

A Strange Land

Tall Christopher Columbus paced the small rear deck. He was worried. He must have missed the isle of Antillia. Why didn't the Asian coastline rise up on the horizon?

He had sailed 2,650 miles in open sea. No explorer of record had sailed this far west. Thank God his three ships had plump bottoms to help them bob in a storm. His flagship, the *Santa María*, rode in the lead. Out on the wings followed the smaller caravels, the *Niña* and the *Pinta*. All told, the crews numbered ninety men.[1] At least two were captain's boys, who were used to fetch and carry things.

No one then knew the true size of the world. The Western Hemisphere was completely unknown in Europe and Asia. In Europe, the North Atlantic had two nicknames: "The Ocean Sea" referred to the known part near Western Europe and West Africa. It

On August 3, 1492, Columbus set sail from Spain in command of three ships—the Niña, the Pinta, and the Santa María—hoping to find a new way to Asia. In this print, King Ferdinand and Queen Isabella appear in the upper righthand corner.

extended as far north and west as Greenland and as far south as to the mouth of the Congo River. "The Sea of Darkness" referred to the vast reaches of the unknown western North Atlantic. Columbus believed it washed up on Asian shores.

His little fleet breasted the waves in an arc. This increased their chances of sighting the Japanese coast. In those days, Japan was called Cipangu. China was called Cathay in the north, and Mangi in the south. The Italian traveler Marco Polo had popularized these terms with his journey in the Far East (1271–1295). He had lived in China for seventeen years. Columbus prided himself on a letter to the Grand Khan (ruler) of China given to him by the Spanish king and queen, who were together called the Crown. The letter served to introduce Columbus as their very high ambassador.

At this time, Spain was not a unified nation. King Ferdinand of Aragon, the large eastern kingdom, had married Queen Isabella of Castile, the large western kingdom. Their political marriage united a broad mid-section of Spain. This union increased the strength of each kingdom.

Castile shared its western border with Portugal. Seaports of both these kingdoms fronted the Atlantic. But the Portuguese had made more of a name at sea, exploring new lands, than the Castilians had. Columbus knew his voyage represented Castile's biggest challenge yet to Portugal to be an Atlantic power, even though Castile's ports of Palos and Cadiz lay recessed from the Atlantic.

Aragon shared its eastern border with southern France. The French vied with Aragon to bring Italian city-states under their rule. It was more a war of words than blood. The French found themselves the natural allies of Portugal. This alliance helped force Castile and Aragon to unite.

The Admiral and His Crews

Columbus was tall for a man from southern Europe, with red hair (getting white at the edges) and blue eyes.[2] His crew tended to be short, with dark hair and dark eyes. Like most Europeans of that day, few could read or write. Columbus had risen to a high level of education for his day. This helped to set him apart from his men. His ambition set him apart even further.

The wealth of Europe had rested in relatively few hands since the fall of ancient Rome. Wealth was mainly concentrated in land. The Roman system of immense estates owned by titled families (nobles) prevailed. Democracy did not exist in Spain—or on Columbus's ships. Columbus was not just in command of his fleet. He hoped, by the power of the Crown's letter, to become the ruler of the new lands he would discover. Never did he dream that one of those new lands would, five hundred years later, become the greatest democracy in the world.

In his youth, Columbus had been a sailor. Now past forty, he had risen far above being a deckhand. He must have dressed the part. His crews did not bathe often or brush their teeth. They trod the boards barefoot, sometimes crunching a roach underfoot. They wore blousy shirts or none at all under a tropic sun. Their knickers sagged at the knees. They slept on deck in two shifts; a night crew replaced the day. They relieved themselves at two iron O-rings hung over the sides of the ship. If their barrels of fresh water turned brackish, the holds were packed with just as many casks of well-preserved wine.

Nobody knows what the real Santa María *looked like. This reconstructed model is a fair estimate.*

Source Document

On losing sight of this last trace of land, the hearts of the crews failed them. . . . Behind them was everything dear . . . country, family, friends, life itself; before them everything was chaos, mystery, and peril. . . . The admiral tried in every way to soothe their distress. . . . He promised them land and riches. . . .[3]

In 1828, American author Washington Irving imagined the feelings of Columbus's crews on leaving the western Canary Islands, off the coast of Africa. His biography of Columbus became popular in the early years of the new nation.

Columbus watched the *Pinta* ride the waves alongside the *Santa María*. The *Pinta*'s captain, Martín Alonso Pinzón, was second in command to Columbus. Columbus preferred to keep the 2,650 miles traveled quiet among the men. He feared they would panic if they knew they were so far from Europe. But by now, a seaman as experienced as Martín Alonso knew. He, too, could read the nautical instruments. How far they had come was sure to slip out to the crews. It was bad enough some had asked to turn back. With each day's sail, the crew's complaints grew.

The universities taught that the world was round. But European universities of that age were rare. They were small, with many part-time students. Cynics said they were noted as much for their students' drinking as for their professors' teaching. Columbus's three crews shared the views of the vast body of poorly schooled people. They thought the earth was flat, lying afloat in space.

The Birds

Each day's sail west now helped Columbus set a new record for open-sea voyaging. The mark for offshore sailing had been broken by the Portuguese. In 1488, Bartholomew Diaz had first located the long-sought South African Cape of Good Hope. His men, however, forced him to return. Diaz's voyage of discovery took sixteen months, covering more than thirteen thousand miles.[4] For much of that journey, he stayed within sight of land.

Now Columbus's crews heard a far-off sound. They all stared at a dark cloud looming up to the north. The keenest eyes made out the oncoming flight of hordes of birds, not in one V shape, but many. The birds kept coming, with a great flapping of wings. No one aboard knew that this was the seasonal migration of North American birds to a warmer climate. Columbus altered his course west southwest to align with the birds.[5]

The flight of varied flocks continued for days. Some of the three crews felt uneasy. On October 10, Columbus's own crew knotted up in a bunch before him. He had heard a whisper that they might cast him over the side.[6] "We have sailed for 30 days," they said. "We must turn back." Columbus's authority was challenged again. "A few more days," he asked. "The birds mean land is close." The seamen reluctantly agreed.

A Mysterious Landfall

The wind picked up and billowed their sails. They were caught in a strong easterly that blew them faster over the unknown waters. They could not have turned back if they tried. They sped westward with the sun.

On October 11, they sighted a floating branch sprouting tropical flowers. Soon they saw more. It surely meant land. At 10:00 P.M. they glimpsed a speck of light in the darkness far ahead. Was it China or Japan? At 2:00 A.M., they made out a patch of white sand. Columbus ordered the anchors dropped. He feared the island might have been ringed with reefs that could have ripped up his ships.

How far had they come from the Canaries? Columbus reckoned 3,466 nautical miles.[7] Later scholars would put the distance at 3,117.[8]

On October 12, by early light, the fleet entered a quiet bay. Small boats carried Columbus and his officers to the beach. They planted the flag of Castile and a cross in the sand. Kneeling, they gave thanks to God. Later paintings would show the Spaniards well shaved and wearing their Sunday best. In reality, at least some of them had to look weather-beaten and in need of a bath and a barber.

Columbus had landed in the middle of a long chain of six hundred islands, the Bahamas. This chain slants down from South Florida toward Haiti. Columbus called his first landfall San Salvador. Scholars still argue as to which Bahamian island it was.[9]

A naked people edged forth from behind trees. They belonged to the major Indian nation in the Caribbean, the Arawak. The Bahamian branch called themselves the Lucayo.

In that first meeting, men of two worlds spoke with gestures more than words. The Spaniards saw some Indians wearing gold nose rings. They traded trinkets for them. A few Spaniards unsheathed their swords to show the Indians. Never having seen swords before, a

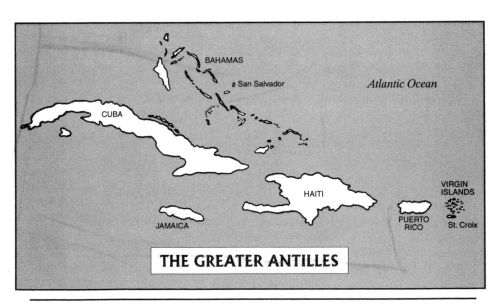

THE GREATER ANTILLES

Columbus's First Voyage landed in the Bahamas island chain. It is thought the first landfall island was San Salvador or one nearby. He then sailed south to Cuba. He followed the coast east to Haiti.

few Lucayo grasped them by the blade. They fast pulled their hands back, bleeding.[10]

Onward to Cuba

Columbus was puzzled. He had not expected to find a naked people. This was not how Marco Polo described Asians. The Lucayo did not even look Asian in any other way. After a rest, Columbus sailed south to nearby islands. He wondered if he was in the legendary seven thousand Spice Islands. Perhaps he should be looking for Java (an Asian island)? But he soon found that the Indians of the Bahamas had never heard of Java. Or of Cipangu or Cathay. When Columbus asked about a major land mass, the Lucayo pointed south.

In time, as Columbus sailed, a shoreline too long to be an island filled the horizon. As the ships drew near, mountains rose up in the interior. "Asia," Columbus and his officers presumed. The Spaniards landed. They soon found small villages with a different type of Arawak people. These were the Taíno. They called their land Cuba. The Cuban Taíno clothed and housed themselves better than the Lucayo. Columbus traded with them for their little gold trinkets. He asked where the gold came from. The Taíno pointed east. Martín Alonso Pinzón's *Pinta* now treacherously sped off east and disappeared to find his fortune first.[11]

A Crippling Shipwreck

The *Santa María* and *Niña* coasted eastward. They crossed a strait at the end of Cuba to a new land. The Indians called it Haiti (Place of High Rocks). The

Haitian Taíno werc friendly and traded with the Spaniards, mainly in small bits of gold jewelry. If Columbus did not know where he was, he had at least found gold.

From his first landfall, he had brought some Lucayo with him against their will. They now begged him to return them to their home island. Columbus ignored their pleas, wanting them to become interpreters for him. In a letter to the Spanish Crown, Columbus wrote:

> I had taken some Indians by force from the first island. . . . they continue to entertain the idea that I

Columbus's first landfall came in the Bahamas.

have descended from heaven; and on our arrival at any new place they published this, crying out . . . "Come, come and look upon beings of a celestial race" . . . [the Cuban and Haitian Taíno] would come out in throngs, crowding the roads to see us, some bringing food, others drink, with astonishing affection and kindness.[12]

On Christmas Eve, 1492, the crews of the two remaining ships drank extra cups of wine to celebrate. Washington Irving would later imagine matters aboard the *Santa María*: "the steersman gave the helm in charge to one of the ship-boys, and went to sleep. . . . while the whole crew was buried in sleep."[13] The current did the rest.

Around midnight, the slumbering men aboard the *Santa María* awoke with a jolt. The ship had struck a reef. In the tidal wash of North Atlantic waves, the bottom of Columbus's flagship was quickly in splinters. He had suddenly lost his flagship. A third of his fleet had gone off ahead. He was left alone in a land he did not know.

Chapter 2

A Boy's Dreams

The known facts of Columbus's life are spare. No living portrait of him exists; all paintings were imagined. Much of Columbus's original writing has been lost.[1] Some survived as copies handwritten by others, and thus were open to changes.[2] Columbus and his family were not above telling tall tales to boost his image. The chief Spanish eyewitness, Bartholomew de Las Casas, wrote about him after Columbus had died. Las Casas worked mainly from his own memories and those of others. All early accounts about Columbus, including Las Casas's, contradict one another in important details.[3] So there is much room for debate in the story of Columbus's life.

Some Columbus biographers enlarged his triumphs.[4] After all, he dared to do what no man dared and he lived to tell the tale. He had discovered an entire hemisphere. In the United States, his admirers put him on a patriotic pedestal not far from George Washington. But the growth of the United States' interest in human rights radically changed the earlier American view of Columbus. He is now often seen as an example of the mind-set of the late medieval world.

Recent scholars point out that Columbus died without knowing where he had been.[5] Columbus also committed dark deeds that suggest a flawed character. For long, these terrible acts were treated lightly. It was said in his defense that Columbus was no crueler than the cruelty of his times.

An Early Wish for a Career at Sea

Christopher Columbus was born in the city-state of Genoa "in or about 1451."[6] (The Italian city-states

These images show how much artists' renderings of Columbus varied from painting to painting.

would not be united as one nation until the nineteenth century.) Like the large islands of Sicily and Sardinia, the northwest Italian seaport of Genoa had come under the control of Spanish Aragon.

Here in Genoa, Columbus's father worked as a wool weaver. The family spoke Spanish at home, which was not unusual for a northwest Italian seaport. Columbus's mother and her parents appear to have been Spanish. His father's surname, Colombo, is Italian. At that time when Jews were being forced to convert to Christianity, Colombo was still a common name among Italian Jews.[7] So Columbus's origins remain obscure. His later writings did nothing to clear them up.

From his father's shop, Christopher and his brother Bartholomew could stroll down to the docks to stare at the ships.[8] Both boys grew tall, with strong arms. At an early age they went to sea as cabin boys. Genoa was a major Mediterranean port. Genoese merchant ships sailed east to the island of Chios in Greece and north to Bristol in England.

Genoa was forced to pay taxes to Aragon. Like Aragon, the French wanted to wring taxes from smaller Italian city-states. Rivalries like this between France and Aragon often made sailing in the western Mediterranean dangerous. Large kingdoms might be in a state of war for years, but never fight a land battle. It was much easier to rake ships at sea with cannon balls.

The attacker might be the French, Spanish, or a

pirate. Or there might be sea battles of rival religions, such as Muslims from North Africa against European Christians. Pirates flew no flag at all. They considered rich passengers from any homeland fair game to be kidnapped for ransom. They might take others to sell as slaves. Whoever sailed the Mediterranean Sea and nearby North Atlantic needed to have cannons on board for their own protection. Christians even enslaved other Christians, and the pope could not stop the practice.

The Way East Blocked

In his early twenties, Christopher Columbus sailed to Chios.[9] The Greek island was a major source of mastic—a multi-purpose tree sap used as a medicine, varnish, and perfume. Chios was also a transfer point to Constantinople (present-day Istanbul, Turkey), where the long overland trade with the Far East began. For long centuries, Muslims and Christians fought religious wars, usually over control of parts of the Middle East, or Holy Land. Beyond Chios, the Moslem Turks now blocked the former rich Mediterranean trade with the Far East. This blockade against Christians had begun with the Turkish capture of Constantinople in 1453.

Since then, the Turkish blockade had dried up prosperity in southern Europe. The pinch was felt most at the western end of the Mediterranean, where Genoa was located. Genoa had once been allied with Venice and Constantinople as a key trading port. Now too many of its ships sat idle. The same could be said for Spanish and Portuguese ports. Their share of shipping trade with the Far East was gone. This made for hard times in Spain and Portugal. Sailors badly needed more cargo to carry to English, Dutch, and Moroccan ports.

A Sea Battle

Lisbon was the principal North Atlantic seaport and the capital of Portugal. It kept up a busy run to the port of Bristol in England. Since the Turkish blockade, the Portuguese had sailed farther west in the North Atlantic than anyone else. They had discovered the Azore Islands by following westward flights of birds on calm, windless days. The eastern tip of the Azores began some 740 miles west of Lisbon. When first discovered, no one lived there.

This island chain lay on the same broad latitude as Lisbon. On most days, strong trade winds called "westerlies" blew out of the west toward Lisbon. Strong currents ran in the same direction. Sailing against wind and current beyond the last known Azore island, where no birds flew west, seemed too risky.

Columbus's first Atlantic voyage was in a Genoese trading fleet of five ships carrying mastic to Holland and England. Off the coast of southern Portugal, the Genoese fleet ran into French warships. Cannonfire blazed back and forth for hours. Three ships sank on either side. Hundreds of sailors died.[10] Columbus followed others into the water as his ship went down.

Wounded, he clung to an oar and paddled toward shore. In this way, he arrived by chance in Portugal. Yet even this story has been questioned as a possible tall tale he may later have invented.

Toscanelli's Idea

There was a large Genoese colony in Lisbon. Possibly with a loan, its residents helped the shipwrecked Columbus settle down in Lisbon. There, he started a small map store. His brother Bartholomew soon joined him. The brothers also took turns sailing as young deckhands to earn enough money to keep their map store going. Columbus sailed on the Lisbon-Bristol run. In later writings, he claimed he even sailed west from Bristol to Iceland. Here, he would have heard tales of an old Viking colony farther west, in Greenland.[11] After four hundred years, it had mysteriously disappeared. The English still had maps showing the southern coast of Greenland just below the Arctic Circle.

Viking explorers in the North Atlantic had discovered America five hundred years before Columbus landed there. They felt Iceland and Greenland were European outer islands. They never thought in terms of a new continent. When the Greenland colony disappeared, around 1450, so did interest in sailing west from Iceland.

The printing press had been invented shortly after Columbus's birth. His parents may have first taught him to read. He patched together the rest of his

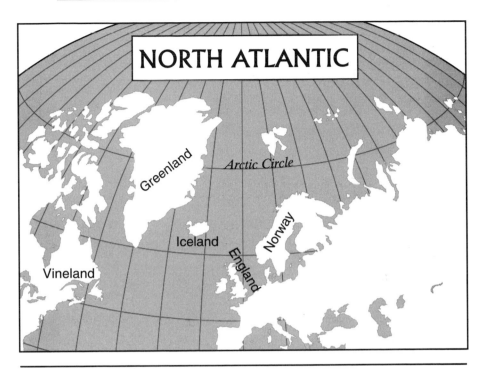

From Norway, Vikings settled Iceland around the year 874. In 982, Eric the Red was exiled to Greenland after he slew someone. Around the year 1002, his son Lief Eriksson sailed west and discovered three new coasts, naming one "Vineland." The exact location on Vineland where he landed remains unknown.

education as best he could. Books, such as *The Travels of Marco Polo*, began to appear at a reasonable price. Columbus marked up his copy.

In Lisbon, he became a part-time student at a local university. Perhaps here he first heard of European theories about a western sea route to the Indies. A leading spokesman of this idea was an elderly physician in Florence, Dr. Paolo Toscanelli. He was also a respected mapmaker.

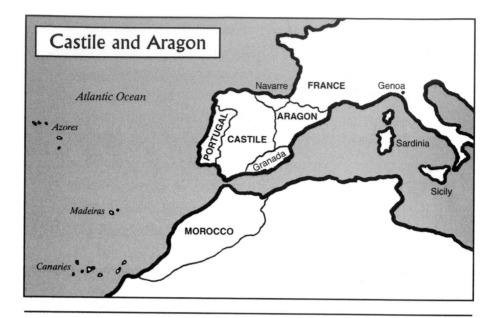

The union of Castile and Aragon strengthened both kingdoms. Portugal was expanding west and south in the Atlantic. Aragon was expanding east to Genoa, Sardinia, and Sicily. Castile followed its rival, Portugal into the Atlantic.

At this time, the limits of sailing in the North Atlantic ran from Iceland down to the Gold Coast of Africa. The next logical step, Toscanelli suggested, would be to sail west beyond the Azores—but not from Lisbon. Toscanelli felt the voyage should be started farther south, in tropical waters. Whoever did so, Toscanelli believed, would reach Cipangu (Japan), and sailing farther west, the Chinese lands of Cathay and Mangi. This new sea route would shorten the overland route to the Far East that had been blazed two hundred years earlier by Marco Polo.[12] It would also circumvent the Turkish blockade.

Columbus fastened onto this idea. He later claimed he corresponded with Toscanelli. But this, too, has been questioned as a possible fib he used to fill out his weak background.

As a boy, Columbus dreamed of a career at sea. If not, he would never have shipped out at around age fourteen. His early naval thoughts had centered about the western Mediterranean Sea. Now Columbus's

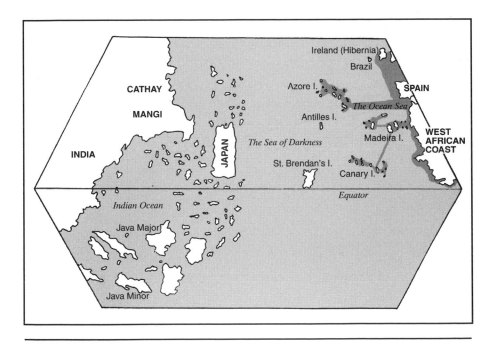

A simplified Toscanelli map shows that the greater part of it was guesswork based on the writings of Marco Polo. The shaded portions are all that was known of Ocean Sea (part of present-day Atlantic Ocean). Notice that North and South America are completely missing from this ancient map because they were not discovered yet.

thoughts shifted to the unknown Sea of Darkness, as the unknown Atlantic was called.

Some European mapmakers were drawing charts about the unknown western Atlantic Ocean. They based their nautical maps on Marco Polo's writings and a long stretch of imagination. Toscanelli's map was typical. Columbus began to regard it as more factual than not. On the map's western half, he could see Japan as a lump of land lying due west of Morocco (in northern Africa). Toscanelli had also drawn the mythical isle of Brazil on his map (vaguely known from a sighting of a strange coast with red trees). Toscanelli placed Brazil off the coast of Hibernia (Ireland). He drew India as immense and China as small. With a lack of adequate maps to prove otherwise, who in Europe could correct him?

Chapter 3

What Was Then Known

The Canary Islands lie offshore from Morocco. Toscanelli estimated that Japan lay about three thousand miles west of the Canary Islands.[1] A more prominent mapmaker, Martin Bchaim, arrived at a similar figure of 3,080 miles.[2] Columbus came up with his own wishful number: 2,400 miles.[3] This meant roughly a thirty-day sail.

Columbus was now a sailor and shopkeeper. He could afford to pay his bills, but he had little money or social standing. Added to this, he was a Genoan fluent in Spanish living as a foreigner in Portuguese Lisbon. But his boyish dreams of a career at sea were about to take him a giant social leap forward.

Into the Noble Class

In his youth, Columbus's red hair and blue eyes were striking features along the Mediterranean.[4] He was

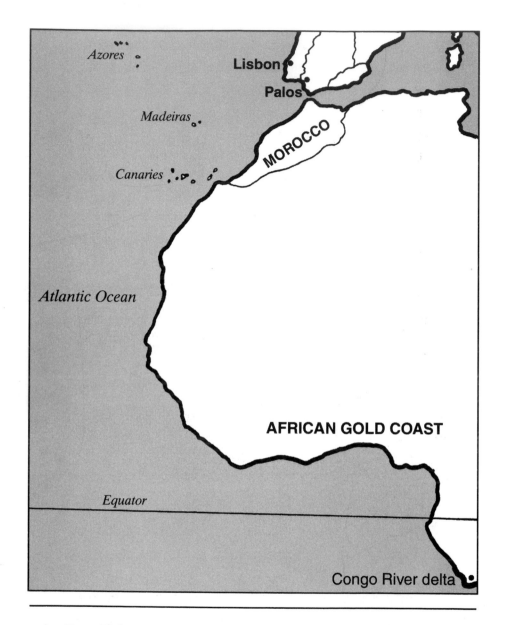

From Lisbon and Palos, the Portuguese pushed south along the African Gold Coast. In 1482, Diego Cam reached the Congo River delta. At first, he thought he had rounded the African cape. This discovery would later be made by Vasco da Gama in 1497.

taller than average, with a long face and a proud bearing.[5] All portraits we have of him are imagined. They show him with Italian or Spanish features.[6] We do not know what he really looked like.

Perhaps his good looks and proud bearing led Felipa Moñiz de Perestrello to marry him in 1479. It was a marriage beneath her class. On her mother's side, Felipa came from a long line of Portuguese nobility.[7] Her father had been an early settler in the Madeira Islands, which lay two days' sail south of the Azores.

With the good fortune of this marriage, Columbus's life changed seemingly overnight. He moved out of his dockside map store and into the noble class. First, he lived at his mother-in-law's manor house in Lisbon. Then he lived at his deceased father-in-law's large estate, three hundred miles out in the Atlantic. He would have no more calluses on his hands from hauling in sails. Now commoners addressed him as "don," a noble title. His new home lay on the same latitude as northern Cipangu, as shown in Toscanelli's map. Here, sugar cane was the dominant crop.

Probably through his mother-in-law, Columbus landed a unique job. From his home in the Madeiras, he became a traveling salesman in the Atlantic. He represented a reputable Genoese trading firm, mainly selling sugar from the prospering Madeira estates.

Columbus sailed down to the African Gold Coast on business. If he truly had sailed to Iceland in earlier years, he would, after arriving on the Gold Coast, have seen the known north-south limits of the North Atlantic. At the same time, he lived on an island in the North Atlantic. Here, his wife bore him a son, Diego, in 1480. Here, too, in the Madeiras, he found writings that had been left behind by his late father-in-law. They told of findings—tree trunks and a human body unlike that of any European—that suggested there was land beyond the western horizon.

In his Atlantic sailings, Columbus spoke with many seamen about how best to cross the Sea of Darkness. In an era of wind-driven ships, the winds, currents, and stars were crucial. What if he sailed south from Lisbon to the Canary Islands, then turned west? Would this put him in the belt of the easterly trade winds? No one had yet tested this newly discovered belt.

Portuguese sea captains kept pushing the known limits of the West African Coast farther south.[8] They traded with local African people, such as the Ife and Yoruba, for gold, ivory, and slaves. Columbus sailed to Portuguese West Africa to sell his goods. He personally saw the Portuguese colony of La Mina in Guinea, founded in 1482 and named for its gold mines.[9] He witnessed Portuguese revenue gained from voyages of discovery, and wondered if he might not do the same.

The Expanding Atlantic

Daring Portuguese mariners had discovered Atlantic islands far to the west and southwest of Lisbon. They had just begun to colonize the West African Coast.

This portrait of a West African king dates back before the Portuguese arrival. It was found in the land of the Yoruba.

They continued their search for the African cape, hoping to round it and sail on to India. But in the meantime, they brought back gold and slaves from Africa. Then, in 1484, a Portuguese sea captain, Diego Cam, sailed a thousand miles farther south down the coast of Africa than anyone before him.[10] He reached the mouth of the Congo River in the South Atlantic, which begins below the Equator. This greatly expanded the known north-south limits of the Atlantic.

It also stirred Columbus to seek an audience with the Portuguese king.

Chapter 4

Bending the Law

The Portuguese king, John II, had recently stabbed a relative to death in a suspected plot to unseat him.[1] This violent incident reflects on the moral climate of the times.

Little is known of the plan Columbus laid before the Portuguese king in 1484. He may have hedged about sailing from the Canaries, because Castile and Portugal had vied for control of these islands. In 1479, they had signed a treaty granting thc Canarics to Castile. Even now, Castile was colonizing the main Canary Islands, south of the Madeiras. Columbus asked the Portuguese king for rich rewards and grand titles beyond what any Portuguese sea captain had ever received.

King John II thought Columbus's price was ridiculous. This man was not even a sea captain or navigator, yet he wanted to be called Admiral of the Ocean Sea. He could not hold a candle to John II's Azores and West African discoverers. So, John II turned Columbus down.

However, there might be some truth to what Columbus said. John II slyly decided to borrow the idea. First, he sent a ship out alone from the Cape Verde Islands. Its sailors took fright and forced the captain to turn back.[2] John II later sent two Portuguese sea captains sailing west out of the Azores. They strove against prevailing winds and currents. They never returned.[3]

Columbus's Wound

Around this time, Columbus's wife, Felipa, died. He seems to have lost his job as well and been left on a weak footing with his in-laws. They seem to have asked him to leave the family home in the Madeiras. Columbus was virtually stripped of his upper-class title of don, which he had gained through his marriage. This reversal of fortune stressed Columbus. It became a deep inner wound. To be poor is one thing. To be poor, then rich, then poor again, is another. One day, he was the most successful member of his Genoese family. The next day, he was borrowing money to keep himself and a small son, Diego, alive.

To add to his troubles, he learned that King John II had stolen his plan. Columbus soon fell into such terrible debt that he feared being thrown into prison. With his son, Diego, then about five years old, he fled across the Portuguese border into Castile. He left the child at a boardinghouse and sought an audience with the Spanish Crown.

It was not easy. It took him a whole year. By then, his clothes were threadbare, his shoe leather had worn thin, and his creditors were hounding him. Perhaps he now began to invent more credits than he had earned to make his offer seem more important to the king and queen.

One day in 1486, Columbus stood before the Spanish monarchs, Queen Isabella of Castile and King Ferdinand of Aragon. They had the power to heal his wounded pride. One of the rewards he would ask for his successful journey would be the title of "don" he seemed to have lost.

The Spanish monarchs were busy fighting a religious war against a large southern province. Here lived the Moors of Granada, the main body of Muslims in Spain. Many of the Moors were descended from North Africans who had invaded Spain eight centuries earlier. The North African Muslims had sought to convert Christians by the sword. The invaders were finally beaten back to the south of Spain, where they had lived now for eight centuries.

King Ferdinand and Queen Isabella wanted to convert all the Muslims and Jews in Spain to Christianity. Occupied with a war against the Muslim province of Granada, Ferdinand and Isabella had little interest at the time in increasing their Atlantic presence. Yet they were annoyed to hear of the constant discoveries being made by the Portuguese along the West African Coast. They turned Columbus's proposal over to a committee for study. Columbus was given a seaman's allowance to live on and then dismissed. He would wait long years for a decision. In the end, the committee voted against him, even though some of its members liked the idea.

The Way to India

In 1488, a new son was born to Columbus, outside of marriage. He named the boy Ferdinand, after the Spanish king. Around this time, a Portuguese sea captain, Bartholomew Diaz, found the long-sought African cape. He named it Good Hope, rounding it at 34 degrees below the Equator.[4] Diaz had mapped the known West African Coast nearly thirty degrees farther south than the Congo delta. It meant that he had found the unknown sea route to India. Some later accounts claimed that Columbus's brother Bartholomew had sailed aboard the Diaz fleet.[5]

In 1491, five years after his first proposal to the Spanish Crown, Columbus stood before their majesties again. Time would have discouraged a weaker man.

He had refined his plan. When asked what rewards he wanted, he demanded a tenth of all goods sent back to Spain.[6] Aside from officially being named a don again, he also wanted the grandest of titles. These were Admiral of the Ocean Sea, Viceroy of the Indies, and Governor of all newly discovered lands.

No Atlantic explorer had ever asked for, or held, even one of these three inflated titles. Not even Bartholomew Diaz. Where did this out-of-work, aging seaman get the nerve to ask such a price? He had never even been a captain or a pilot on a major sea voyage. Again Columbus's proposal was rejected by a committee. It cited his grandiose demands as cause for rejection. Still, some on the committee liked the idea itself.

To Unify Spain

Ferdinand and Isabella wanted to unite all of Spain. The kingdoms under the Spanish Crown held a majority of Christians but a large minority of Jews. The ratio may have been about four to one, Christian to Jewish. The Jewish presence in Spain was ancient, and had already passed through its Golden Age.[7] The second largest minority, of Muslims, or Moors, had never really been accepted by the Christians. The massive Muslim invasion to convert Christians forcibly in the eighth century had never been forgotten.[8] Yet, after eight hundred years, the Jews and the Moors of Spain were now some of the most learned and successful people in the country.

A Focus on Converts

Spain held well over a million people who were non-Christian. The Spanish Crown made every effort to force them to convert to Christianity. But even when minorities converted, the Christian rulers remained suspect that their conversion was only for show.

People were seized on suspicion of straying from, or helping others to stray from, state-approved forms of worship. A convert under suspicion could be thrown into jail for saying a type of prayer that varied from the approved norm. Spain became a police state. This solidified the powers of the king and queen. The religious police were called inquisitors. They could enter suspects' homes at any time, question people, determine their thoughts, seize them, imprison them, torture them, seize their property, and even kill them

For very serious crimes, a prisoner might be stretched between four horses. After blood was drawn, by whip or cuts, four horsemen pulled the prisoner's limbs in four directions until they were torn off.

in horrible ways. These practices created a reign of terror known as the Spanish Inquisition.

Commoners, Nobles, and Kings

The Crown and the landowner nobility, with their huge estates, lived lives of enormous privilege. They tried to stay on good terms with one another. As the Crown enjoyed more raw power than the nobles, the nobles sought to limit the Crown's power and increase their own. The Crown resisted. The common citizens in Spain had no rights or voice in government. They did not have freedom from unreasonable search and seizure—or of press, speech, assembly, and fair trial. Under the Spanish Inquisition, they did not enjoy freedom of religion, either.

The Riots

Through the centuries, commoner rabble rousers sometimes stirred up the uneducated street mobs. They led poor Christians in deadly riots against wealthier non-Christians. A long line of Spanish kings found it convenient not to punish these religious riots, even though they involved murder and theft. It seemed better to let the street mobs riot against Muslims and Jews than to have them riot against the king. The riots also served as a warning to Muslims and Jews that the law did not protect religious minorities. The law existed mainly to protect the privileged class.

For centuries, Spanish street rioters went unpunished.[9] King Ferdinand and Queen Isabella followed the example of earlier Spanish kings in siding with street crowds that rioted against non-Christians. The Spanish mobs especially targeted the converts, or conversos, known as New Christians. These were mainly Jews who felt forced by state policy to convert to Christianity. The New Christians often held important positions. Many converts publicly became Christian, but kept some of their old forms of worship in the privacy of their homes. As New Christians came to number about three hundred thousand and more, they troubled Ferdinand and Isabella the most. Some New Christians had grown influential enough to join in the nobility's struggle for more rights.

Ferdinand and Isabella now bent the law further in their goal to unify Spain. They increased spying and questioning by the inquisitors. Converts whose prayers and answers diverged from accepted Christian practice were punished. The Spanish Inquisition became the cruelest version of a milder policy then in effect in Italian city-states. Valuables seized from victims enriched the treasuries of Castile and Aragon. This helped the Crown, especially since Ferdinand and Isabella had bankrupted their kingdoms fighting the religious war with the Moors and with their constant skirmishing at sea with their Christian European neighbors.

The Chief Inquisitor was Tomás de Torquemada. In his torture chambers, thick dungeon walls muffled the nightmare screams of converts whose religious practices had been found to be at fault. One of

Torquemada's leading advisors told him what to do with those minorities who refused to convert. He suggested killing them all.[10] At the very least, he recommended expelling them from the country. This would mean a total of some six hundred thousand people to be killed or exiled. Ferdinand and Isabella chose expulsion from Spain as the appropriate punishment. As they decided this, early in 1492, Castile and Aragon at last conquered the Moors of Granada. In the terms of surrender, the Spanish Crown promised that they would not expel the Moors. It was a promise they would soon break.

A Change of Mind

Ferdinand lost interest in Columbus. He withdrew his half of the Crown, the kingdom of Aragon, from considering Columbus's plan, which was now called the Enterprise of the Indies. The Spanish king set his mind on gaining more influence along Italian shores. He was a prime mover in seating a Spaniard as the new pope. Rodrigo Borgia won the papacy through underhanded political tricks.[11] He took the name of Pope Alexander VI. As pope, he became famous for his misdeeds, including fathering children by his mistresses. He came to symbolize the low moral climate of the times.

Queen Isabella of Castile, on the other hand, listened to the advice of the few people at court who believed in Columbus. She called Columbus back as he was leaving the country on a mule, no doubt to

The Spanish Inquisition investigated suspects and forced many to change their beliefs. Some were tortured, and those who refused to change were sentenced to die by burning.

escape debtor's prison. He stood before the queen again, bewildered. He felt himself a ruined man. To his amazement, the queen said she had changed her mind. She might back his plan. He needed only to soften his demands.

It is easy to imagine Columbus agreeing at this point. Why not accept 5 percent instead of 10, and less fancy titles? Instead, Columbus became a stone wall. Yes, he was penniless and had made no prior discovery at sea. Yet he would not give in on the high titles and the high rewards he felt he deserved if he were successful in his plan. He would not back down on his demands. It then took three months to finalize a contract.[12] Columbus seems to have worn down the queen's council.

The final agreement granted Columbus his lavish 10 percent of all goods returned to Spain as a result of his discoveries. It restored him to the nobility on his own merit with the title of don. It also gave him the

Source Document

. . . under the first inquisitor-general, Tomás de Torquemada, in the course of fourteen years (1485–1498) at least two thousand Jews were burned. . . . He was so hated that he lived in constant fear of death. . . . When Torquemada went out, he was attended by a bodyguard (Familares) of fifty, and two hundred foot-soldiers, to protect him from assault. His successor, the second inquisitor-general, Deza, erected still more scaffolds. . . . Spain, under the wrath of the Holy Inquisition, became literally a scene of human slaughter. . . . nearly all the European princes, and even the parliament of Paris, bitterly blamed the perverseness of Ferdinand and Isabella. . . .[13]

This description of the Spanish Inquisition comes from the nineteenth-century German historian Heinrich Graetz.

high-sounding titles of Admiral of the Ocean Sea, Viceroy of the Indies, and Governor of all lands he found. This last title implied that he would be judge and juror of all his subjects in those lands. He would sail under the banner of Castile. Merely by his signature, which he began to mystify with occult symbols, he legally became a noble again.

On August 3, 1492, Columbus set sail from Palos (on the southeast coast of Spain) in a fleet of three ships. The harbor was crowded with Jews who refused to convert. Perhaps three hundred thousand were being expelled at all Spanish ports and border crossings. Many would be robbed at sea or in new lands. An estimated equal number of the Jewish converts, or New Christians, remained behind, as the principal target of the Spanish Inquisition. These injustices were an ironic note to the great discovery Columbus was about to make. His discovery would lead, in time, to the United States, which would come to represent freedom and human rights to millions.

A Drab Fleet

Just about everyone knows the names of Columbus's three ships. Columbus commanded the *Santa María*. Martín Alonso Pinzón, a leading ship owner from Palos, captained the *Pinta*. His younger brother, Vicente Yañez Pinzón, captained the *Niña*.

The Pinzón brothers had picked out most of the crews from their hometown of Palos. Other Pinzón relatives and friends sailed with them. Some seamen

Christopher Columbus set sail from Palos to the hoots and howls of the angry townspeople.

of Palos had recently been caught withholding part of the Crown's share from a previous fleet's voyage to Morocco. Queen Isabella found this a good excuse to penalize the town of Palos to pay for two of Columbus's three ships. The townspeople of Palos considered this fine unjust. Citizens came down to the dock to hoot at Columbus as he sailed out the Tinto River with his drab fleet. They regarded him as an unfair expense wrung out of them in hard times. This added to the bedlam down at the docks as Columbus's fleet set sail.

Where in the World Was He?

Columbus's First Voyage crossed the Atlantic, landed in the Bahamas, coasted along northern Cuba, and then northern Haiti. Columbus's flagship crashed into a dangerous reef off Haiti on Christmas Eve, 1492. Historians assume the crew was too drunk, considering it was a holiday, to do anything before the damage passed beyond repair.

The wreck of the *Santa María* placed Columbus in serious jeopardy. The bottom of his largest caravel was ripped open. This loss meant he did not have enough shiproom to return to Spain with all his men. Meanwhile, Martín Alonso Pinzón had deserted the fleet, racing ahead on his own. The shipwreck and sudden treachery now made Columbus vulnerable to attack by the far more numerous Haitian Indians. But the local Taíno chief, Guacanagarí, put Columbus's anxiety to rest. He lent Columbus enough Indians to unload the *Santa María* onto shore. As Columbus wrote to the Spanish Crown: "So loving, so tractable, so peaceable are these people, that I swear to your Majesties, there is not in the world a better nation, nor a better land. They love their neighbors as themselves; and their discourse is ever sweet and gentle...."[1]

The Taíno seemed so friendly that forty of Columbus's crewmen volunteered to stay behind. Like Martín Alonso, they, too, wanted to get their hands on small gold nose rings and earrings before the Crown's

Columbus discovered that the Taíno of Cuba and Haiti lived in tropical huts clustered in villages.

men would arrive on a new voyage to keep records of the wealth being discovered. Columbus salvaged wood from the *Santa María* to build a blockhouse. He christened the settlement "Isabella" and renamed Haiti "Hispaniola."

Into the Open Sea Again

Columbus transferred to Vicente Yañez Pinzón's *Niña*. Then he coasted east looking for the missing *Pinta*. He came upon Martín Alonso's ship in a cove. Strong easterly winds had snapped its mast. Since Columbus was a Genoese among the Spanish seamen of Palos, he scolded Martín Alonso only mildly.

Once the mast on the *Pinta* was repaired, Columbus captained the two ships to the end of Haiti. He veered sharply to the northeast into the Atlantic to reach the belt of the westerly trade winds. This caused him to miss another large Taíno island across from Haiti, Borinquén (present-day Puerto Rico).

The returning two ships sailed into a blinding storm that lasted several days.[2] When the skies cleared, Columbus found the *Pinta* nowhere in sight. He sailed for the nearest of the Azores. That way, if his ships never returned, his discovery would still be known. Reaching the island, he sent half his crew ashore to give thanks to God for their safety in the local church.

The settlers of this Portuguese colony reacted badly to the news of Columbus's success on Spain's behalf. They took the Spanish sailors prisoner. After five days, Columbus somehow succeeded in getting them released. Then he set sail again.

A second storm blew him toward Europe with frightening speed. He would have crashed into the Portuguese cliffs north of Lisbon had not some night clouds parted to allow him to glimpse a wall of land ahead.

The Amazing News

On landing, Columbus announced his discovery to the local Portuguese. He claimed he had found a sea route to the Indies. This news traveled by horse to King John II in Lisbon, even as Columbus tacked south for Lisbon to make much-needed ship repairs. King John II wondered what to do. Should he imprison Columbus on false charges or kill him and his crew?[3] If he silenced Columbus, he could then send his own ships to claim this new land for Portugal. Nobody in Castile would be the wiser. But word soon reached John II that a second ship from Columbus's fleet had landed in northern Spain. Martín Alonso, blown far off course north of Portugal, was in the Spanish Bay of Biscay. This meant that news of Columbus's discovery was speeding overland to Ferdinand and Isabella. John II saw he could do nothing underhanded. He allowed Columbus a safe haven in Lisbon.

From Lisbon, Columbus sailed on to Spain. He arrived on March 15, 1493, at Palos. He had been gone six months. Martín Alonso had to sail completely around the length of Portugal to reach Palos. His battered ship came limping up the Tinto River shortly after Columbus had docked. Martín Alonso had to be carried off the *Pinta*. He was deathly sick from the fierce storms. Days later he died.

News of a westward sea route to the Indies made Columbus an instant hero in Spain. He traveled across the width of Castile and Aragon to meet with the king and queen in Barcelona. Street crowds hailed him and the Lucayo Indians he had brought back. At last, he stood before King Ferdinand and Queen Isabella once again. They could not have been more delighted with him. Dukes and counts came forth to clap the wool weaver's son on the shoulders.

Columbus paraded before them the exotic samples he had brought back. These treasures included a small pile of gold nose rings, a gold mask, pearls, Indian corn, sweet potato, a better type of cotton than the kind grown in Europe, tobacco leaves, and tasty Indian cassava bread. Columbus showed off iguanas and brightly colored parrots (unknown in Europe) in cages. Lastly, several Lucayo Indians appeared at his call, almost naked. They sat down cross-legged with lighted cigars, blowing blue smoke into the air.

For the entire court, these were true wonders to see. It seemed that, through Columbus, the Spaniards had beaten Portugal at its own game of Atlantic discovery. Now Spain, too, had a colony west of Lisbon, one with gold. Columbus had not lost a single man in the sea journey, except for Martín Alonso, who died after its return. That could not be held against Columbus.

Columbus became the sudden favorite of the Spanish Crown and their court. He was popular with the crowds in the street as well. For decades, the Spaniards had heard about the new gains made by daring Portuguese sea captains in the Atlantic. Now here was a strong blow struck for Spanish pride. Columbus took it all as his rightful due. The high opinion he always held of himself suddenly seemed justified.

The Second Voyage

New monies had to be found to bankroll a much larger Second Voyage to reap the rewards of Columbus's discovery. No one representing the Crown had been aboard Columbus's risky First Voyage. The Crown could not be sure it was getting its full share. The sailors had certainly socked away plenty of smaller bits of gold. Obviously, a high authority had to be placed at Columbus's side to watch him. He was already too costly to the Crown and was personally deeper in debt than ever from his borrowings for the First Voyage. For this task, the Crown chose a hard man of the Inquisition, Juan de Fonseca. His job would be to spy on Columbus during the Second Voyage and oversee the precise measurement of shares of gold. As agreed before the First Voyage, the Crown would receive 90 percent and Columbus 10 percent.

A fleet was put together of the finest ships in Spain. It took five months for all the financing and preparations to be completed. On September 25, 1493, Columbus left the harbor of Cadiz on his Second Voyage.[4] He stood high on the rear deck no doubt dressed to fit his grand title of Admiral of the Ocean Sea. He surely took great pride in the sixteen ships that followed his own. Including their crews, the seventeen ships held between twelve hundred and fifteen hundred men.[5] Some were soldiers sent by the Crown. These men were not crossing the Atlantic to found a

Source Document

Ferdinand and Isabella bent all their energies to the work of fitting out an expedition for taking possession of "the Indies." First, a department of Indian affairs was created, and at its head was placed Juan Rodriguez de Fonseca, archdeacon of Seville. . . . Fonseca was all-powerful in Indian affairs for the next thirty years. . . . He was one of those ugly customers who crush, without a twinge of compunction, whatever comes in their way. The slightest opposition made him furious, and his vindictiveness was insatiable. . . . The cost of the present expedition was partly defrayed with stolen money, the plunder wrung from the worthy and industrious Jews who had been driven from their homes by the infernal edict of the year before.[6]

This excerpt is from John Fiske, a leading United States historian of the nineteenth century who specialized in early American history.

colony. They wanted to get rich quick and come home fast.

The adventurers came from every walk of life. Circumstance threw them together pell-mell, regardless of social class. Rich sons of landowners, soldiers of fortune, grizzled sailors, and ne'er-do-wells all rubbed elbows during the crossing. They were being transported in floating boxes with sails to an unmapped

King Ferdinand and Queen Isabella, pictured together in this woodcut, ruled Spain during Columbus's voyages.

island far across the sea. There was not a woman was among them. Ship hygiene was terrible.

Columbus sailed first to the Canary Islands. From there, he set a more southerly route west than he had on his First Voyage. Luck was with him. He struck the easterly belt of trade winds at their most favorable point. This whisked his fleet across the Atlantic. Everyone on board marveled at his skill. Later scholars would say he had abandoned nautical instruments and relied now on know-how, instinct, and guesswork.

Was He in the Missing Antillia?

On November 3, 1493, Columbus's seventeen ships approached an unknown island well southeast of Haiti. He saw Indians on the beach running away from his fleet. Their skin was darker than that of the Taíno or Lucayo. They wore headdresses of the brightest parrot plumage. They bound their upper arms and legs with cotton string to flex the muscles. As the Spaniards landed, the Indians fled into the woods. In their village, Columbus and his men found what looked like human body parts in their clay cooking pots—a thigh here, a forearm there.

Columbus coasted north to nearby islands, only to find much the same. The Spaniards freed some of their Taíno captives. The Spaniards then casually took others they freed as their own slaves. This was the first direct enslavement of American Indians by Europeans, except for Columbus's kidnap of some Lucayo from his first landfall.

Columbus passed on, curving northwest to a thick cluster of islands. He called them the Eleven Thousand Virgins.[7] Today, we know them as the Virgin Islands. On one of the main islands, St. Croix, a random canoe suddenly appeared with several dark-skinned Indians. They boldly fired arrows at the Spaniards.[8] A naked young woman stood up in the canoe and shot an arrow that passed through the shield of one Spanish soldier.[9] The arrowhead was barbed, so that it could not easily be removed without tearing flesh.

Columbus would hear more about these darker Indians, the Carib. He named their region after the mythical isle of Antillia on Toscanelli's map. Columbus was actually in the Lesser Antilles, having passed from Guadeloupe into the Virgin Islands chain. When at last he reached the eastern tip of Haiti (which he called Hispaniola), his wounded soldier died.[10] Apparently, the arrowhead with which he had been shot was tipped with a slow-acting poison. Columbus went ashore to bury the man. The first death of the expedition had a solemn effect upon the others.

Chapter 6

People of the Americas

Historians estimate that between 10 million and 15 million Indians lived in the Americas in 1492. The old view held that they were descended from a series of wanderers, over the course of thousands of years, who had crossed a frozen land bridge at Bering Strait. It was believed that Bering Strait was the sole gateway from Asia into the Western Hemisphere.

We now know more about the North American glaciers. Two vast Canadian ice sheets long blocked the land route south from Alaska to the United States. Around 11,000 B.C., a western corridor opened up. It connected Bering Strait to Montana.[1] But by then, Indians already lived in the Americas. How did they get here?

Multiple Entrances

The new view is that they came in many migrations and by varied routes. Some came by sea, others by land bridges, still others by land bridges and then by sea. Early skulls found in the Americas show traits of different early people.[2] The three oldest campsites in North America were excavated not on the Pacific Coast, but on the Atlantic. They include Meadowcroft, Pennsylvania (15,000 B.C.); Cactus Hill, Virginia (14,000–16,000 B.C.); and Topper, South Carolina (10,000 B.C.).[3] The oldest campsite in South America was found on the Pacific Coast of Chile (10,500 B.C.). Another site in Peru is almost as old.

American Indian Civilizations

From hunter-gatherer beginnings, American Indians built three major empires in Mexico and Peru. The Maya, Aztec, and Inca civilizations at their peaks enjoyed better public health measures than much of Europe in 1492. These advanced Indian civilizations often buried their kings in pyramid tombs, as in ancient Egypt. The Maya perfected a calendar more accurate than those used in the rest of the world. The Aztec had orders of knights, as in King Arthur's England, and a capital city of around two hundred fifty thousand people. The Inca excelled at engineering highways, mummifying royal corpses, and surgically repairing skulls broken in war or by accident. Above all, these three American Indian civilizations enjoyed more prosperity than Spain, Portugal, or England in the age of Columbus.

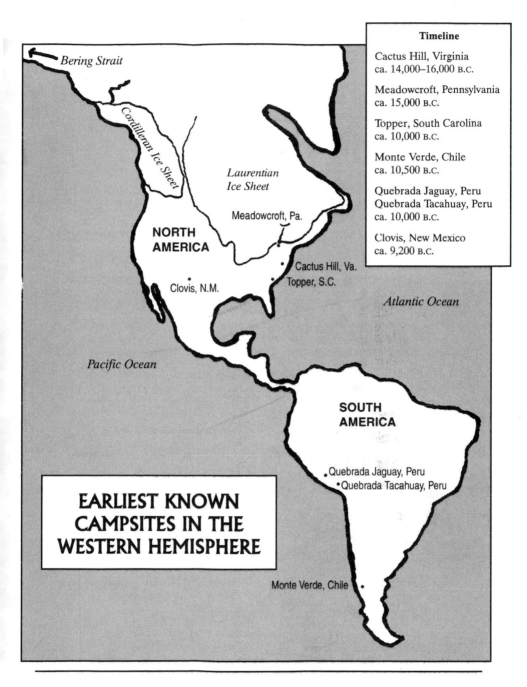

Timeline

Cactus Hill, Virginia
ca. 14,000–16,000 B.C.

Meadowcroft, Pennsylvania
ca. 15,000 B.C.

Topper, South Carolina
ca. 10,000 B.C.

Monte Verde, Chile
ca. 10,500 B.C.

Quebrada Jaguay, Peru
Quebrada Tacahuay, Peru
ca. 10,000 B.C.

Clovis, New Mexico
ca. 9,200 B.C.

Bering Strait

Cordilleran Ice Sheet

Laurentian
Ice Sheet

Meadowcroft, Pa.

**NORTH
AMERICA**

Cactus Hill, Va.

Topper, S.C.

Clovis, N.M.

Atlantic Ocean

Pacific Ocean

**SOUTH
AMERICA**

Quebrada Jaguay, Peru
Quebrada Tacahuay, Peru

**EARLIEST KNOWN
CAMPSITES IN THE
WESTERN HEMISPHERE**

Monte Verde, Chile

A long passageway opened up between the Cordilleran and Laurentian Ice Sheets near the end of the Ice Age, allowing people to migrate and settle in to what is now North and South America.

The Caribbean Basin

By 1492, the island Arawak (divided by dialect as Taíno, Lucayo, and others) and the island Carib populated the Caribbean islands.[4] They arrived by dugout canoe from South America. The island Arawak lived a pleasant life in the Greater Antilles and the Bahamas, where farming and fishing were easy. The mainland Arawak thrived in Venezuela and were more numerous.

The island Carib came from their jungle homeland in equatorial Brazil. They may have been the bravest people, who volunteered to leave when food supplies ran low. This advance guard developed a hard core of brave warriors. They differed from more peaceful Carib who also came into the Lesser Antilles.

The island Carib were found from north of Trinidad to Guadeloupe.[5] They sent out raiding parties to capture Arawak. Their original name was Canibale or Caribale.

From 300 to 900, the Classic Maya built their cities around templed ceremonial centers. This is a museum drawing of a Mayan temple at Tikal, Guatemala.

A British artist, John White, drew coastal Indians in Virginia around 1585. White's Indian medicine man may closest resemble what the mainland Arawak looked like.

From them we derive the words cannibal and Caribbean.

In Columbus's early contact with the island Carib, he referred to the region as "the Caribbee Sea." This term later became applied to the entire Caribbean Basin. Columbus had no idea how small the ratio of Carib to Taíno was in the Caribbean. The island Carib may have only numbered between thirty to fifty thousand, compared to close to 2 million island Arawak.

The most populated island, Haiti, held about a million Taíno in 1492.[6] In 1496, Bartholomew Columbus took a rough census to tax the Indians of Haiti. He counted 1.1 million over the age of fourteen on half the island.[7] The Haitian Taíno generally lived in districts away from the ocean, to be safe from Carib raids. Villages inside their districts averaged one thousand to two thousand Indians.[8] The Taíno grew cassava, sweet potato, squash, pineapple, Indian corn, peppers, cotton, and tobacco. Cassava bread was the main staple. It took a long time to grow, required little work, and could be preserved for months.[9] Fruits abounded, including star apple and guava berries. The sea provided manatee, fish, and turtle to eat. The island Taíno also ate the meat of large iguanas, small dogs that could not bark, rodents, and a variety of birds. The island Taíno on Puerto Rico, Cuba, and Jamaica may have added an additional six hundred thousand to the population of Haiti.[11]

Columbus had built his first settlement, La Navidad, at the edge of the district of Cibao. It was the

Source Document

The habits of these Caribbees are brutal. . . . In their attacks upon the neighboring islands, these people take as many of the women as they can. . . they eat the children which they bear to them. . . . When they take any boys prisoners, they dismember them . . . and then when they wish to make a feast they kill and eat them. . . .[10]

Dr. Diego Alvarez Chanca, a physician on board Columbus's Second Voyage, gave this chilling account of Carib cannibalism in a letter to authorities in Spain. Some modern scholars believe Chanca came to this conclusion too quickly. They suggest that the Carib may have raided the Arawak to carry off brides—not primarily for cannibal meals.

smallest Taíno district on Haiti.[12] In the interior at Maguana, a larger district, an unusual Carib ruled over the Taíno. His name was Caonabó. He had been chosen as chief of Maguana for his great strength. He came from the north-coast villages of mixed Arawak-Carib, the Macorix.[13] Though he lived among the Arawak Taíno, Caonabó retained the fiery spirit of the island warrior Carib. He would become a heroic figure in the natives' struggle against Columbus and his men.

War With Caonabó

After burying his dead soldier on the eastern tip of Haiti, Columbus led his seventeen-ship fleet west along the coast. He approached the settlement of La Navidad after dark. Columbus shot off bombards as a sign he was back. A dead silence followed. Since it was late, no Spaniard from the fleet went ashore until the light of morning. When they arrived, they found a shocking scene. As historian John Fiske described it:

> The fortress was pulled to pieces and partly burnt, the chests of provisions were broken open and emptied, tools and fragments of European clothing were found in the houses of the [nearby] natives, and finally eleven corpses, identifiable as those of white men, were found buried near the fort. Not one of the forty men who had been left behind in that place ever turned up to tell the tale.[1]

The chief of Cibao, Guacanagarí, lived four miles inland. He sent word to Columbus: The Spaniards at

La Navidad had fought among themselves with knives. One had even killed another. They had outraged the Indians by taking whatever they pleased in gold and women.[2] The Spaniards carried their outrages beyond the limits of Cibao into the interior, as far as the borders of Maguana. They had split into factions, weakening their already small numbers. Caonabó then rose up and killed those Spaniards just outside Maguana. Next, he marched the 110 miles to La Navidad with his warriors and wiped out the little Spanish colony. The last Spaniards swam out into the rough swells of the Atlantic and disappeared.

A Foothold in the New World

Columbus's seventeen shiploads of men took this news hard. They had barely recovered from the burial the day before of the Spanish soldier mortally wounded at St. Croix. Now they learned of more Spaniards slain. They had arrived in the Lesser Antilles in a giddy state. Finding Spanish bodies in the bush in gruesome decay sobered them quickly.

It was too depressing to stay at La Navidad. Columbus buried the dead and doubled back about seventy miles. Bad winds drove him into a bay. It was no easy matter, as ferny marshes dominated the shoreline. He had passed out of the small district of Cibao. In this new bay, he founded a second settlement, naming it Isabella.

Isabella lay at the edge of a huge and fertile plain. The Spaniards would call it the Vega Real (Royal

Plain). Deep beyond this vast meadowland lay a new hilly Taíno district. The Spaniards called it the Vega. They assumed Cibao was a huge district that extended into the mountainous interior and that it also held gold mines. This gave rise to a phrase rich with lure at the settlement: "the golden mountains of Cibao." In reality, the Indians knew of no mountains that yielded gold, and Cibao was actually quite small.

Columbus envisioned building a town of two hundred thatch-roofed huts surrounded by strong fortifications. Instead, three hundred to four hundred of his men fell sick, many with stomach cramps. In the heat and humidity, more men soon came down with fever and extreme fatigue. The settlement of Isabella took on the look of a battlefield hospital. The sharp class differences among the men now came into play.

The hidalgos, or hereditary nobles, refused to do any manual labor. They considered it beneath them. These men with titles going back for generations complained that Columbus, a Genoan and a commoner, had just been handed his titles. The horsemen would not allow their horses to be used to pull anything heavy, such as stones to build a wall. The sailors and soldiers did not take to tilling the soil. Barroom rowdies, ruffians, and vagabonds made their presence felt. They all began to get on each other's nerves. Nothing much got done.

Columbus now saw that this chance harbor was not a good one. But too many of his men were ill to relocate. They complained that they did not have enough large stones in this marshy site to build a protective wall encircling the settlement. Under the tropic sun, they were often coated with a film of sweat just sitting still. Few of them wanted to work in such heat.

The Crown's chief man, Archdeacon Fonseca, took note of all this. He had help in keeping a close eye on Columbus. One, a priest of Aragon, was Ferdinand's spy. He would report only to the king. Another was the commanding officer of the troopers, Pedro Margarit, also from Aragon. Fonseca took under his wing as well a popular young hidalgo, Alonso de Ojeda, who had been a swashbuckling captain in the war against the Moors. Groups of gripers began to form on their own. The frequent bite of gnats and mosquitoes made matters worse.

The Admiral of the Ocean Sea was lost on land. Despite his fancy title, he was still a sugar salesman and a sailor. He could not mold his men into productive teams. All his questioning of the Haitian Indians failed to locate the gold mines. Columbus still had no idea where he was. If these were the Antilles, then where was Japan? At one point, Columbus boldly marched into the rainforest with four hundred men suited in armor. He followed the Yaké River, as mountain gold washed down into riverbeds. Some one hundred miles inland, near the headwaters of the Yaké, he built a fort. He named it Santo Tómas, after the doubter among Jesus Christ's Apostles, as a way to shame the gripers. Columbus left Margarit to guard the fort with fifty-six soldiers. On this trip, Columbus found small bits of low-grade gold in a few Indian villages. But the Indians could not say where the gold came from. Columbus returned to Isabella disheartened. He found some of his men so rebellious that he hanged the worst of the offenders. These were the first Spaniards to lose their lives by his order.

Columbus Turns Slaver

The damp heat was fast spoiling the Spaniards' food and rotting their wine casks. Columbus decided to send twelve ships back for more Spanish foodstuff (cows, pigs, wheat, and barley). He felt this would help reduce the sickness crippling his colony. Unfortunately, he found he did not have much gold to send back to the Crown. It came in such flimsy bits that it made a poor pile. His men were constantly squirreling gold away when Fonseca was not looking. As one member of the expedition wrote of the constant stealing of small items of gold: "whoever got caught was well whipped; some had their ears slit and some the nose, which was very pitiful to see."[3]

Now Columbus took a major step in the history of the Americas. It would be as critical as his first landfall. He ordered a roundup of some fifteen hundred Taíno. He had the force of arms to do it against unarmed local Indians. Columbus loaded five hundred Indians on ships to be sold in the slave mart in Spain.[4] When no more could be crammed into the ships' holds, he told his men to pick out slaves from the rest. In short, he

71

began to treat the Indians as property and revenue. Interestingly, the Taíno villages had no Taíno slaves.

This was the first European mass seizure of American Indians for the purpose of selling them into slavery in Europe. It came early in Columbus's Second Voyage, and opened the door to the worst instincts among the Spaniards. Following the example set by their leader, the Spaniards became increasingly abusive to the Indians.

Columbus may have been thinking like a Genoese sea merchant, in terms of cargo to fill the holds. But when the cargo became human, he crossed a historic line. From then on, it was a crime to be an Indian on Haiti.

The Spaniards had come to the Americas with the Spanish Inquisition in their baggage. They were now simply unpacking. The authority of Archdeacon Fonseca and his priests lent weight to this policy. The models of masters and slaves created by the Portuguese at La Mina and the Spaniards on the Canary Islands formed Columbus's guidelines. The Spaniards also believed they had a right to do whatever they pleased with the Taíno. They believed their superior Christian faith and better weapons gave them this right.

Columbus wrote an apologetic letter to the Crown describing the Taíno slaves he was sending back instead of gold. He claimed they were cannibals, although they were not. He even attempted to cast his act in a light of securing "the welfare of their souls."[5] Perhaps to soothe his own conscience, he asked that the Taíno be treated better than other slaves in Europe (who were mainly captives from piracy at sea, debtors of all faiths, or blacks from a small African slave trade). Then Columbus packed the five hundred Taíno tightly into the storage holds without any concern for their welfare. A third of the captives died on board; many others died soon after landing in Spain.

Spaniards physically abused and tortured the Taíno to force them to work in mines and fields.

The Dream Bubble Breaks

Ever bewildered by not knowing where he was and by the problems caused by the gripers, Columbus fled in three ships on a voyage of exploration. He sailed along the southern coast of Cuba almost to its western tip. He convinced himself that this was the Asian mainland. Then he sailed south to Jamaica. He was surprised to find it an island much smaller than Haiti.

Like Columbus himself, his officers did not know where they were. But they did not believe they were in Asia. Still, Columbus ordered them to sign a paper stating that they were. The document added that, if they said otherwise, their tongues would be slit. Then, although there are no clear reports, it seems as if something snapped inside Columbus. He suffered a breakdown. For a while, he lay near death. He would be an invalid for five long months.[6]

The Siege of Ojeda

Meanwhile, young Ojeda had relieved Captain Margarit as commander at the fort of Santo Tómas. From here, Ojeda led bands of Spaniards deep into the lush rainforest in search of gold. He was a small man and a show-off. To punish an Indian for a slight offense, he sliced off the ears. With Fonseca's backing and the prestige of his own frontline captaincy in the Spanish war against the Moors, Ojeda took a leadership role among the men in Columbus's absence.

Ojeda's bands roved in the direction of the mountainous country of Maguana, which they mistakenly called Cibao (believing Cibao was larger than it was). Some rode on horseback. Others trod on foot. The name of the chief of Maguana, Caonabó, meant "Lord of the Golden House." Learning this, the Spaniards imagined there was much gold in these mountains. However, they found only small bits of jewelry in the scattered Indian villages. Without any authority to curb them, they grew more abusive to the Indians. Soon they were committing broadscale rape and theft.[7]

Hearing of these abuses, Caonabó flew into a rage. He and his men attacked a nearby band of Spaniards and killed them. Then Caonabó returned to his hammock to rest. When Ojeda heard of the slain Spaniards, he was in the fort. He sent word to all the roving bands of Spaniards in the rainforest to join him. The fort had a tower and a moat around it.[8]

Caonabó learned that the Spaniards had gathered at the fort near his district. He put out a call for warriors from all his villages in Maguana. An army of more than a thousand Indians assembled. They dabbed on red war paint, then marched to the Spanish fort. They were amazed when they first saw the tower and the moat. The Taíno surrounded the little fort. Each charge brought heavy casualties, until Taíno bodies littered the moat. The Taíno were unfamiliar with the military tactic of siege warfare. But Caonabó figured it out fast. If he just kept his men encircling the fort, he knew the Spaniards would soon run out of food and water.

Ojeda had prepared for a siege by stocking plenty of supplies. He soon noted that, by the second week of the siege, Caonabó's warriors began to slip off after dark. They returned home to sleep in their hammocks. The Taíno never fought at night. They believed too many spirits roamed about in the darkness. Seeing the Indian desertions, Ojeda rode forth in starlight cavalry charges, killing scores of Indians each time. Caonabó found he did not have enough men to maintain a siege and withdrew.

Ojeda and his men returned to Isabella to brag about their victory. There, they witnessed the return of Columbus's three ships. They—along with Fonseca and the gripers in the colony—saw Columbus carried off his ship, delirious. Word passed around that

Source Document

He was slight of body but very well proportioned and comely, handsome in bearing, his face good-looking and his eyes very large, one of the swiftest men. . . . He was very devoted to Our Lady. . . . He was always the first to draw blood wherever there was a war or a quarrel.[9]

Bartholomew de Las Casas wrote this description of Alonso de Ojeda.

Columbus had nearly died at sea. This further weakened the line of command at the colony.

Margarit's Desertion

In Columbus's absence, his brother Bartholomew had arrived with the supply fleet. Just before this, even before Columbus left Isabella to explore the Cuban coast, a message had come from Captain Margarit. The fort was about to be attacked by Caonabó. Columbus had sent seventy men to help defend Santo Tómas.[10] Young Ojeda led them. However, no Indian attack came.

Ojeda and Margarit had broken up into squads and raided Taíno villages. They kidnapped young Taíno boys as slaves. This was how Ojeda had come under siege. It appears that just before the siege, Margarit had received a message from Columbus's youngest brother James, nicknamed Diego. Diego was mild and studious, much more out of place on this island than his seventeen-year-older brother Christopher.[11] On hearing of Spanish atrocities, Diego had sent word to Margarit to stop them, scolding him. Margarit and his troopers, away from the Crown's spies, were most likely collecting bits of gold and hiding them in their belongings. Captain Margarit was a tough man who commanded all the gruff soldiers. He felt insulted when a young pup like Diego Columbus scolded him. Leaving Ojeda to man the fort, Margarit returned to Isabella seething.

Margarit fast gathered the worst of the Spanish rebels around him. If they had stolen sizable amounts of gold, this was the time to get away with it, before they could be searched. What better opportunity than to seize the very ships that had brought Bartholomew to Isabella? Margarit and his men clambered aboard and set sail before they could be stopped. They planned to present themselves to the Crown as Spanish patriots eager to report on the mismanagement of the colony.[12]

Ojeda Breaks a Truce

Five months after he fell ill, Columbus stood on his feet again. He decided a force had to go back into the interior to capture Caonabó. Ojeda volunteered. To Columbus's surprise, Ojeda rode off with only ten horsemen, all armored head-to-foot.

News had reached Ojeda that Caonabó admired him for his strong defense during the siege. Ojeda now sent word ahead by Indian runners that he wished to speak with Caonabó. He asked for safe passage. It was granted.

Ojeda traveled deep into the mountain country. Here, he met with the chief of Maguana. Ojeda told Caonabó that Columbus wished to make a peace treaty. He said that Columbus would give Caonabó a huge bell that fascinated all the Taíno. The Indians marveled over how, when the bell rang, the Spaniards came forth from their huts to go to their chapel. The Indians called it the talking bell. Caonabó highly prized such a gift. The Taíno believed it truly came from the heavens, even if the Spaniards themselves had not.

Caonabó assembled an army of two thousand Taíno to accompany him to Isabella. The mass of Indians trailed behind Ojeda and his horsemen. At a rest stop by the Little Yaké River, Ojeda showed Caonabó a pair of blue-steel handcuffs. He explained that the king of Spain wore these bracelets when

Under Ojeda, the Spaniards won a decisive victory over a large Taíno army in Haiti. This engraving shows a battle more typical of Florida or Venezuela, where the Indians fired arrows from long bows. The Taíno mainly used darts fired by small crossbows.

arriving on horseback at an important meeting. He asked if Caonabó would like to wear them. Caonabó said yes. He felt deeply honored. Ojeda offered the chief his own horse to ride. He helped Caonabó up into the saddle. In a flash, Ojeda jumped up in front of the handcuffed Carib chief and clutched him tightly. He and his men then sped off at a gallop.[13]

Caonabó soon lay in shackles at Isabella. Ojeda returned to the fort in the interior with a sizable Spanish force. Caonabó's wife, Anacoana (Golden Flower), and his brother assembled an army of more than seven thousand warriors. They marched on the fort. Ojeda led his cavalry forth and surprised them. He saw how unwieldy the Indian army was on uneven terrain. It broke into five divisions across wood and plain to surround him. Ojeda did not wait for an attack. Where a lesser man might have turned back to the fort, Ojeda made bold cavalry charges. He hit the Taíno at the weakest points of the Indian army. He slew hundreds and even captured Caonabó's brother. First some, then more, then this whole large Indian army fled.[14]

A lesson was learned on both sides. The Taíno could not win a pitched battle against the Spaniards, no matter how big their numbers. Spanish lances and swords were too punishing on their bare flesh. The Taíno weapons—mainly darts—could not penetrate steel armor.

Still, there would be more battles to come.

Chapter 8

No Fair Trial

After his exploration of Cuban and Jamaican waters, Columbus sailed west no more. He had all he could do to manage his health, the colony at Isabella, and Fort Santo Tómas. Illness still riddled his colony, but to a lesser degree. The men were eating more food from Spain, grown in Isabella's fields. Taíno slaves tended those fields, under Spanish guard, and many sickened and died from their captive labors. They had never known such hard work in their hot humid climate. Their own fruit trees and cornfields and cassava plants required only the mildest effort.

Columbus was glum. The Spanish Inquisition had produced a country of spies at home. A whisper from an angry neighbor into the right ear could cause an arrest. Not surprisingly, Columbus found himself surrounded by spies in this Spanish colony. A sizable number of men had already deserted under Margarit to blame him for all the colony's problems. Young Ojeda was brave, but was acting overly reckless in the interior. The hundreds of thousands of Indians on the island only needed a good spark to explode. If they managed to wipe out Ojeda's small troop, they would march next on Isabella, where a third of the men seemed to always be ill.

Columbus went about daily, checking on the cultivation of wheat, the building of the stone fortifications, and the dredging of the harbor. He also wrote brooding letters in his own defense against letters sent back to Spain by others attacking him. In this regard, Fonseca had become his worst enemy.

The Gold Tax

The Columbus saga had peaked with his discovery of a hemisphere he failed to comprehend from these few islands he had seen. Columbus's rapid rise to fame was, from the moment he returned to Haiti, in decline. His settlement was a disaster. He was freely seizing Indians as slaves, both to ship back to Spain and for his own local use. He did not have enough little bits of gold to send home in a sizable pile. When he learned that his slave cargo was largely dying on the long journey to Spain, he grew desperate.

Columbus now laid a harsh tax on the Indians. Every native of Haiti over the age of fourteen had to pay him a few ounces of gold or its value in goods every three months.[1] To help position his tax collectors, Columbus built more forts fanning out from Isabella. Those Indians who paid the tax were given a symbolic receipt to wear around the neck. Those who did not pay, Columbus ordered hunted down. Their hands were chopped off. Many of those punished bled to death.

As Bartholomew de Las Casas would later report, there were too many Indians on the island and not enough known sources of gold at this time. Thus, the gold tax could not really be paid.[2]

When the Taíno failed to pay Columbus's gold tax, he had them hunted down and tortured.

Columbus feared the tales Margarit and his fellow deserters would tell in the Spanish court. Their testimony would support the letters from Fonseca and others saying that he mismanaged the colony. Columbus decided it was time to sail home to refute all charges against him. He would leave his brothers Bartholomew and Diego to run things in his absence. Just then, Indians searching for gold to pay the unjust tax discovered a gold mine on the south shore. Columbus advised his two brothers that, if the gold mine proved to be a good one, they should move the colony from Isabella to the south shore. Then he set sail. Caonabó lay in chains below deck, intended for the Spanish slave mart.

Stuck at Sea

Columbus set a course farther south than before, in the hope of sighting new islands. Instead, in spite of his talent for dead reckoning at sea, he languished for months in calm waters. There was no wind to drive his ships forward. The Admiral of the Ocean Sea was stuck, as if glued to the water. The Spaniards on board, reduced to severe rations, came close to eating the Taíno captives in the hold. Given the least water, the Indians died the fastest. Caonabó and most of the other Taíno ended up being dumped into the ocean.

Back in Spain, this near cannibalism by Spaniards added one more horror story to all the rest. On his return, Columbus found the Crown deeply disappointed in him. The king and queen had received many letters of complaint about him and had met with Margarit in person to hear his attacks on the Columbus brothers. The Crown now refused to hear Columbus's side of the matter. They believed his day in the sun was over. With no riches coming in from the new colony, they lost interest in Columbus. The colony was not worth what had been spent on it so far. The Crown's coldness took the form of a two-year silence. Columbus stayed in Spain, retired against his will.

New Veins of Gold

Meanwhile, Bartholomew Columbus found that the new gold mine seemed promising. He sailed to the south shore and discovered a deep-water bay thirty miles from the gold mine. He moved the colony of Isabella there, naming the new settlement Santo Domingo. With forced Indian labor, he worked the gold mine. Slowly, he discovered new veins of gold elsewhere. In a crude census of half the island, he estimated that there were 1.1 million Indians.[3] He sent that figure home to Spain, along with larger piles of gold that held chunks of ore.

This new information woke up the Crown to their chronically mismanaged colony. King Ferdinand in particular seems to have changed his mind often over Columbus's botched plan to sail to Asia. Now he grew eager. The Crown called Columbus in to discuss a possible new voyage. Columbus was more than happy to comply.

However, not many Spaniards wanted to take their

By 1498, King Ferdinand had more reign over the new colonies in the Indies than Queen Isabella.

chances in the New World now. The word was out of the many hazards they would face. This meant that only low-grade crews could be rounded up. They numbered about two hundred, with about a dozen convicts, including murderers, to fill out the lot. Two of the convicts were women. The Crown was well aware by now that life was cheap in the Indies. Why should they send dashing young nobles into danger? It seemed far wiser to have nobles stay at home to enforce Ferdinand's hold over his Italian subjects, such as Sicily. Ferdinand also needed the nobility to enforce the Crown's massive purge at home against non-Christians. He was planning to break his treaty with the Moors and force them to convert or be expelled. He knew many valuables could be seized.

A New Continent in the Wrong Place

On May 30, 1498, Columbus began his Third Voyage. He was now about forty-seven years old. He chanced on a southern course that led his six ships, once again, into a windless zone. After a sweltering passage, he reached a new Lesser Antilles island, naming it Trinidad. Sighting a large coastline on his left, he followed it. To his amazement, he came to the multiple mouths of a huge freshwater river. The strong flow of the river suggested that it came from a continent, not just an island. The great river was the Orinoco. The continent was South America. This new finding bewildered Columbus. There was not supposed to be a continent here.

Just beyond the Orinoco, Columbus came to a sweeping arm of land that curved up into the Caribbean Sea toward Trinidad. He sat propped with pillows on deck, suffering from a crippling gout (a severe swelling of the joints, especially in the toes) and an infection of the eyes so bad they bled. He stayed on board while a landing party went ashore. They returned to tell how the local Indians were clothed in pants and skirts and lived in larger houses than had been seen on Haiti. They spoke a similar language to the Taíno. They called themselves Arawak, and their land, Paria. Many wore pearls, obtained by Indian divers from pearl beds to the west.

Sailing a little farther west (along what is today eastern Venezuela), Columbus found the mainland heavily populated. Las Casas would estimate it held 2 million people.[4] Without setting foot on this new land himself, Columbus dubbed it the Pearl Coast. Then, still sick, he sailed for Haiti. His brothers Bartholomew and Diego had much bad news to tell him.

Problems Multiply

Before his departure, Columbus had named one of his aides, Francisco Roldán, as chief justice in the colony. The intent was to let Roldán hang rebels, instead of Bartholomew doing it, so that the gripers could not blame Bartholomew. Roldán had cozied up to Christopher Columbus to win just such a promotion. When Roldán forgave the worst of the colonial rebels after Columbus had left, they came under his wing.

Source Document

. . . we were soon visited by a great number of the inhabitants, who informed us that the country was called Paria, and that further westward it was more fully peopled. . . . I found [it] . . . one of the most lovely countries in the world, and very thickly peopled. . . . [the Parians] are very graceful in form,—tall, and elegant in their movements, wearing their hair very long and smooth, they also bind their heads with handsome worked handkerchiefs. . . . These people are of a whiter skin than any that I have seen in the Indies. . . . Their canoes are larger, lighter, and of better build than those of the islands . . . and in the middle of each they have a cabin or room, which I found was occupied by the chiefs and their wives.[5]

In his letter to the Crown, Columbus described the mainland Arawak his men found in South America.

In Columbus's absence, Roldán planned to kill Bartholomew and seize the governorship of the colony. But Bartholomew learned of the treachery before Roldán could carry it out. Roldán fled to the far northeast with some seventy Spaniards. Here, he persuaded the Vega Taíno to join him. No doubt he promised them more benefits than he intended to give.

Aside from a tenth of the island now in revolt,

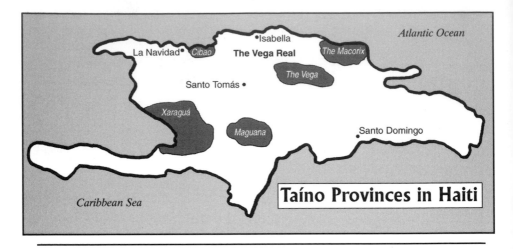

A reconstructed map of Haiti in earliest colonial times. Borders of the Taíno provinces are crude estimates. These districts were ruled by caciques, a Taíno word for chiefs. (Much later, the island would be called Hispaniola and become divided between Haiti and the Dominican Republic.)

other rebel factions sprang up. Some imitated Roldán and seized small territories of their own. Others inside Santo Domingo plotted against the remaining Columbus brothers, Bartholomew and Diego. The only peaceable part of the island was Xaraguá in the southwest. Here, the chief, Behechio, and his sister, Anacoana, reigned. They reluctantly paid the Spaniards' tax in great shiploads of cassava, cornmeal, sweet potato, cotton, and other goods. No gold could be found in their province.

Columbus saw how his colony problems had multiplied. Even among those loyal to him, the men kept pocketing concealable bits of gold, especially in powder form. The Crown's spies could not keep up with the theft. The colonists also drank Spanish and Indian wine heavily. The frequent drunkenness led at times to knifings. By now, most of the hidalgos were gone. Fonseca may have departed as well. The gripers now seemed to be in the majority. To make the situation worse, Indian resistance had also stiffened in some remote parts of the island.

Two years of turmoil passed. The Crown barely paid attention to the complaints of Columbus or his men who returned, some with slit noses as punishment for stealing. Sufficient piles of gold and exotic Indian goods kept coming in by the shipload. Isabella now had worries about Columbus's enslaving the Taíno and shipping them to Spain. Ferdinand, however, was more interested in taxes from his Italian subjects, such as Genoa and Naples. He was glad to have the gold Columbus sent, to use to strengthen his military forces.

The Plantation System

In time, the colony rebels exhausted Columbus's patience. He decided to pacify Roldán, who represented the gravest threat. Roldán wanted to own the choice grasslands of the immense Vega plain as his own estate. Columbus granted his wish. Implied in the grant were the Indians living there as well. In short, with this treaty, Columbus introduced the plantation system to the Western Hemisphere. The plantation system dated back to Roman times. It required the labor of tenant-farmers or slaves to make it work.[6] The next three hundred fifty years would see many plantation masters and slaves in Western Hemisphere history.

By now, Columbus and his gold tax had destroyed much of the Haitian economy. The main foodstuff—cassava—all but grew by itself, but it took a long period of time. Many of the island's cassava, sweet potato, and cornfields lay abandoned. The Taíno were deserting their villages to hide from the Spaniards in the island's wilder parts. As their food supply dwindled, some lived day-to-day on whatever luck brought them.

A Sea Captain Surpasses Columbus

In 1497, Vasco da Gama sailed for Portugal down the West Coast of Africa. His four ships rounded the Cape of Good Hope and tacked up the East Coast. He then followed the route of Arab dhows (raft-like boats with sails) east for twenty-three days to cross the Indian Ocean. He landed at Calicut, in southern India. Da Gama's crews numbered around one hundred seventy men. Only fifty-five would survive the long trip home.[7]

Da Gama reached Lisbon in 1499. The news of his fabulous voyage stunned Europeans. They now realized the world was much larger than Europe. Da Gama's voyage of discovery also put Columbus's First Voyage to shame. It measured an estimated thirty thousand nautical miles—ten times longer than Columbus's First Voyage.

Da Gama brought the same attitudes to India that Columbus had brought to the Caribbean. At first, he offended the Indians. He offered them cheap trinkets, the normal items of trade along the West African Coast. Then he mistook them for Christians, as nothing was known of Indian religion in Europe. When he later sailed to India again with a larger fleet, he acted true to the European heritage of wars of religion. On learning that a big Muslim dhow was returning to India from a religious pilgrimage, and was defenseless, he stopped it. He stole the pilgrims' money, then burned the dhow, drowning three

How the Indians of Calicut received Vasco da Gama can only be imagined. Little in writing survived.

Source Document

The city of Calicut is inhabited by Christians. They are of tawny complexion. Some of them have big beards and long hair, whilst others clip their hair short or shave the head, merely allowing a tuft to remain on the crown as a sign that they are Christians. They also wear mustaches. They pierce the ears and wear much gold in them. They go naked down to the waist, covering their lower extremities with very fine cotton stuffs. But it is only the most respectable who do this, for the others manage as best they are able.[8]

Vasco da Gama's brief journal records the most significant events of his first voyage. It is believed that this was an early European encounter with the strict Hindu caste system.

hundred eighty Muslims on board, including women and children.[9] He also hanged some Hindu fishermen, then butchered their bodies and sent the pieces ashore. He suggested that the Indian ruler eat them. Luckily for him, the local ruler in India did not become enraged and retaliate.

Columbus Comes Full Circle

Da Gama's success spelled doom for Christopher Columbus. The Spanish Crown no longer believed in him. They now commissioned Alonso de Ojeda and Vicente Yañez Pinzón to sail separately to the Pearl Coast and gather riches. This breached the Crown's contract with Columbus, which gave him exclusive rights of exploration. When Ojeda and Pinzón reached South America, they committed the same atrocities as Columbus had committed in the Caribbean.[10] In two voyages, Ojeda explored the Pearl Coast farther west than Columbus had, attacking the mainland Arawak culture. Pinzón seems to have charted more coastline, from Costa Rica down to southern Brazil. However, little is known of their adventures.

In 1500, the Spanish Crown also sent a new stern governor to replace Columbus. Francisco de Bobadilla had been handpicked by Archdeacon Fonseca, Columbus's old enemy. Bobadilla was a man who easily lost his temper. Since Fonseca's return, when he had spoken out against Columbus, Fonseca had been promoted to bishop for his supposed good work in Indian affairs. The truth was that, under his command, barely an Indian had been converted to Christianity. He had overseen terrible outrages against the Indians without making any strong objection.

Bobadilla arrived at Santo Domingo in August 1500. He had worked himself up into a tizzy over all the bad things he had heard about Columbus. His mood grew fouler when he was greeted by seven Spanish corpses strung up by the dock. The dead were colonists who had rebelled against Columbus. Five more rebels were languishing in the local jail.

Columbus and Bartholomew were each off on separate expeditions in the interior. They were fighting Indians.

The colony had grown to a thousand armed Spaniards. They were "none too savory a lot," as one historian wrote; many had slit noses and ears, the sign made in Spain to mark prison inmates for life.[11] Bobadilla freed the Spanish rebels from jail. He led them to Columbus's house and, in a fit of wrath, they

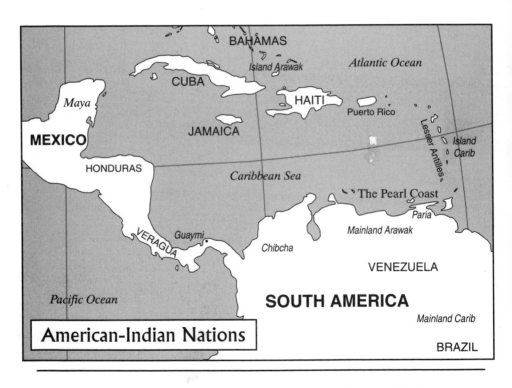

The first American-Indian nations affected by Columbus's discovery were the island Arawak and mainland Arawak of Paria. In time, Columbus fought the Guaymi, and Alonso de Ojeda and Francisco Pizarro fought the Chibcha. Later, Hernando Cortés conquered the Maya and Aztec in Mexico.

destroyed all the papers they found. These included invaluable charts Columbus had made of the Caribbean islands.

Columbus and Bartholomew returned separately from the interior. Bobadilla had each man seized and thrown in jail, along with their younger brother, Diego. Thus, Columbus's Third Voyage ended in his disgrace. The Admiral of the Ocean Sea and Viceroy of the Indies soon lay in shackles on a ship headed for Spain. He was sent back as a convict, on the mere word of Bobadilla. Like many of the Indians he had maimed or killed, Columbus had received no trial.

Chapter 9

In Search of Columbus

Once Columbus was in Spain, the Crown let him lie in chains in a Spanish prison for six weeks. They suspended his share of the gold and produce from the Indies. When they finally summoned him before them in late November 1500, they put on a stern face. Columbus could not hold back his tears.

The king and queen took pity on him. This man of arrogant pride was now humbled. He fell to his knees. Ferdinand and Isabella did not want to hear his defense, however. They ordered his 10 percent share from the Indies to continue and forced him to retire.

To their dismay, they soon received severe complaints against Bobadilla from the Spanish colonists. This time, no blame could be attached to the Columbus brothers. Meanwhile, Isabella had grown more worried as Ferdinand grew more dominant over his Italian provinces. Isabella regretted allowing Taíno slaves into Spain. At her bidding, the Crown decreed an end to slave trade from the Indies. Isabella had even sent some Taíno slaves back in the Bobadilla fleet. After that, however, the decree was not enforced. When Isabella died, in 1504, it was discarded. Ferdinand profited from it most. A year after Isabella's death, he married the niece of the French king. He was now at his peak as a power in European politics.

The Wealth Stream

Gripers returning from the Indies complained that Bobadilla was a madman and that the Indians were dying of starvation. King Ferdinand knew little of the colony's troubles on the island. He cared even less. Chief Guacanagarí of Cibao—who had helped Columbus at first—now wandered the interior in grief and in search of food.[1] Had no wealth flowed into Spain from the Indies, Ferdinand might have similarly wrecked the Spanish economy. The expulsions of well over half a million Jews and Moors who would not convert had caused a major brain drain on his country. The policing of another half a million Jews and Moors who had been forced to convert to Christianity taxed his resources at home.

Then came word of gold discovered in the Haitian north. The news swept through Spain. The wealth stream from the Indies was flowing again.

In February 1502, the largest Spanish fleet to the Indies sailed from Cadiz, led by Nicolas de Ovando. It carried twenty-five hundred excited adventurers, in addition to crews who manned the thirty ships. Among them came young Bartholomew de Las Casas, a New Christian from a converted Jewish family.[2] He would become a friar in 1510. He would make his mark on history as a true voice of Christian conscience in the New World.[3] His father had been an early adventurer in Columbus's Second Voyage.[4]

Las Casas would go on to speak out against the excessive violence of European arms against a defenseless native people. His writings came to be labeled "the Black Legend." One of his manuscripts was not published for three hundred years.[5]

An Epidemic of Suicide

After sending Columbus back to Spain in chains, Bobadilla raised the level of Spanish cruelty in the Caribbean. For the first time, there were reports of Spanish attack dogs ripping out Indian intestines. Las Casas described a Spanish policy of taking one hundred Taíno lives for every Spaniard the Taíno killed. The Spaniards roasted Indians alive, hung them from gallows, massacred a whole village, even wagered on who could slit a Taíno in two the fastest.[6] These atrocities did not occur on Columbus's watch, cruel as his was. The Indians of Haiti now began to commit suicide by poison or hanging at an epidemic rate.

The Short Route to India

As new Indian gold filled the Spanish treasury, Ferdinand called in Columbus again. Maybe Columbus could find a second Hispaniola? Columbus was over fifty years old and ailing. Yet he seized upon the chance to return to the New World. He proposed finding a shorter route to India than da Gama's. Ferdinand gave Columbus four battered ships pocked by worm holes.

Those Spaniards who wanted to go to the Indies at this time had already sailed with Ovando's fancy fleet. Nobody wanted to go with Columbus and his salvage-yard wrecks. A lot of gangly boys in their late teens, some from orphanages, were rounded up to fill out his crews. Columbus took Bartholomew with him and his son Ferdinand, then thirteen.

The Storm God Huracán

In the "Caribee Sea," Columbus saw dark clouds and heavy swells approaching. He recognized them as signs of a bad tropical storm. The Indians called it Huracán, after one of their gods. Columbus made for Santo Domingo, the only port within reach. King Ferdinand had forbidden Columbus to land here, so as not to interfere with Ovando. But Columbus felt he had no choice. At the port's mouth, Columbus could count twenty-four ships in Ovando's fleet unfurling their sails for the trip home.

Columbus sped a message to Ovando. He warned of a storm of great intensity and asked for safe harbor.

Ovando refused. Columbus found a nearby inlet to ride out the hurricane. He watched Ovando's return fleet pass by in proud majesty. Each ship lay low in the water, loaded down with cassava, sweet potato, and cornmeal, as if carrying most of the island's food away. In far lesser quantity, they carried the most precious cargo, buckets of gold.

The twenty-four ships barely cleared the horizon when winds with the force of a tornado struck them. Twenty ships went down, carrying to their deaths Bobadilla and Roldán (who was returning home to be named a don). Three ships staggered back to Santo Domingo, in ruins. A fourth ship made its way feebly toward Spain. Interestingly, it held Columbus's share of plundered gold and produce.

Landlocked

Columbus repaired damage to his four ships and sailed on. He navigated the rough stretch between Cuba and Jamaica, then came to a strange coast. He had found Honduras, with its hump of a cape. Local Indians advised him that no strait existed west or north. In doubling back on the cape, Columbus sailed into fierce gales. He and his crews fought beating wind and rain for a month. He described it as grueling. It nearly killed him.

Once he was in calm waters again, Columbus coasted south. He came upon the Indians of Costa Rica and then the Guaymi of Veragua (Panama). All wore more gold ornaments than the Taíno did, almost

The Toltec-Maya Indians of Yucatan replaced the Classic Maya of the southern jungles. Their main cities lay at the western end of the Caribbean five hundred miles north of Columbus's Honduras landing.

---

entire breastplates. The same problems now arose as on Haiti. Columbus's crews abused the Indians and the Guaymi revolted. A bloody battle broke out. Spanish falconets (small cannons) drove the Guaymi back.

The Admiral Beached

Columbus now knew that no strait existed from the Honduran cape to the Pearl Coast. But he had found a new source of gold, Panama. He had to scuttle (destroy) two ships that were too worm eaten. He crowded his crews onto the other two. They nearly sank off Jamaica. Here, he suffered his most humiliating shipwreck. He would remain for a year. With Bartholomew's help, he countered mutiny and threat of Indian warfare.

Back on Haiti, meanwhile, Ovando increased the level of cruelty practiced by Bobadilla. He invited eighty Indian chiefs to a peace feast in Xaraguá, the most tranquil part of the island. As the chiefs were dining, Ovando's armed men sprang upon them. They bound the chiefs and burned them all alive, except for Anacoana, Caonabó's wife. Ovando hanged her from a tree. One of his aides, spurred on by bloodlust, rode about slicing the legs off small children.[7] With this treachery, Ovando destroyed Indian organization on the island. The failing Indian economy was now in ruins.

In June 1504, a ship from Santo Domingo rescued Columbus. He arrived in Spain close to Isabella's death. Ferdinand dismissed his stories of gold in Veragua. Columbus brought too little of it home. His crews may have pocketed much of it.

The Pickle Dealer

Aging Columbus was now a small multimillionaire by modern standards. Still, he did not own a huge landed estate, as the hereditary Spanish nobles did. Grown cranky, he thought he should be richer. He filed complaints of being shortchanged on his accounts. In 1506, he died without knowing what he had discovered or

Through treachery, the new governor, Ovando, captured the leading chiefs of Haiti. He burned them alive. He spared only Anacoana, hanging her instead.

where he had been. His death went almost unnoticed. His invaluable journals later disappeared. No statue would be erected to him in Spain for three hundred and fifty years.[8]

Spanish rabble kept arriving on the Pearl Coast. It was now called Venezuela (Little Venice), as waterfront Arawak towns on Lake Maracaibo, built on stilts, resembled the Italian city of Venice. Ojeda's chief aide on this expedition was a swineherd who could not read or write.[9] His name was Francisco Pizarro. He would, in time, through the same treachery as the other Spaniards before him, conquer and loot the Incan Empire, the richest in the Americas. This would in time become the greatest theft of all.

But first, Ojeda was wounded in Colombia. This region, southwest of Lake Maracaibo, bordered on the Chibcha nation. They were among the best goldworkers in the Americas. Ojeda had been struck with an arrow he feared had been dipped in a delayed-action poison. He left Pizarro in charge while he sailed in search of a doctor at Santo Domingo. After suffering severe hardships on his journey back to Santo Domingo, Ojeda died there in great pain in 1509.

Also taking part in ventures with Ojeda and Pinzón was a pickle merchant from Seville who became a maritime explorer, Amerigo Vespucci.[10] He knew the aging Columbus. He had helped outfit some of the ships used in Columbus's later voyages. They had even lived in the same house in Spain for a while.[11] Vespucci may have seen Columbus as a mentor. Like Columbus, he made an astonishing social climb from pickle dealer to ship's pilot through the need for men of daring in the New World. Like Columbus, he, too, may have told a few tall tales to promote his career.

After Columbus's death, a claim was made that Vespucci had explored the new southern continent from the Pearl Coast down to Brazil. It is not clear whether Vespucci really did this, merely said he did it, or sailed under the command of Vicente Yañez Pinzón.[12] The claim took on a life of its own, helping Vespucci gain the position of pilot-general of Spain.

Afterward, a few maps appeared showing the

Amerigo Vespucci's first name came to be associated with two continents, but nobody is sure if it was deserved.

known northern half of South America with the name America. Nobody then knew there was a North America. In 1541, a famous cartographer named Gerard Mercator drew the first crude map of the Western Hemisphere showing two distinct continents.[13] He labeled one "AME" and the other "RICA," as a variation of Amerigo. This labeling nailed down Vespucci's name to the Western Hemisphere. Some scholars believe Vespucci never deserved it.[14]

The Myth and the Man

Two schools of thought slowly developed about Columbus. Las Casas's writings were kind to the admiral, but damned the outrages of the Spaniards in general. A second school arose under Gonzalo de Oviedo. A hidalgo, he had been a king's man in the Indies, measuring out the Crown's share of gold and produce. Between 1535 and 1557, Oviedo published a history of the Indies.[15] It looked favorably upon the Spanish conquerors, and promoted Columbus as a world hero. It was completed fifty years after Columbus's death. It was more slanted to Spanish pride than to the outrages reported by Las Casas.

The Oviedo school prevailed over Las Casas for centuries. Future American writers as diverse as Washington Irving and Samuel Eliot Morison would lean in its direction. They, too, saw Columbus as one of the truly great movers of history.

The Oviedo and Las Casas accounts disagree on

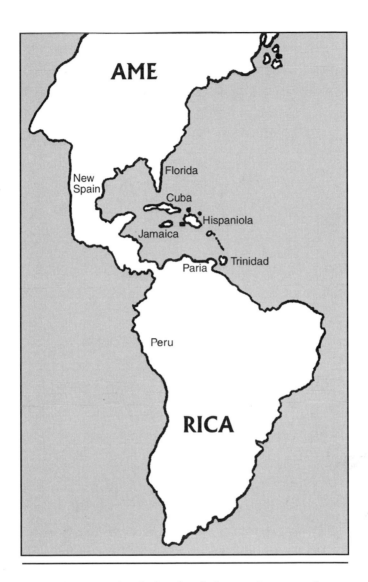

This is a brief sketch of the crude map of the Western Hemisphere made by Gerard Mercator in 1541. It was the first use of the word "America" on the two continents that were yet to be fully charted. Mercator placed part of the word on each continent.

Source Document

Every step of the white man's progress in the New World may be said to have been on the corpse of a native. Faith is staggered by the recital of the number of victims . . . the heart sickens at the loathsome details of barbarities recorded by the friar Bartolomé de las Casas. . . . A selfish indifference to the rights of the original occupants of the soil is a sin which lies at the door of most of the primitive European settlers. . . . In 1515, Las Casas, moved by the spectacle of human suffering, returned to Spain, and pleaded the cause of the injured native in tones which made the dying monarch [Ferdinand] tremble on his throne.[16]

This was the opinion of William H. Prescott in his 1837 first book. Prescott would go on to become the principal historian writing about Spanish conquests in the New World.

many points. Columbus and his son Ferdinand left writings that disagree with Oviedo and Las Casas on too many points. This left many of the facts of Columbus's life in question. Modern scholars today speak of separating the man from the myth. The process is not yet complete.

In 1790 came an accidental discovery of an old copy of Columbus's journal of his First Voyage.[17] It lent more weight to the Oviedo view of Columbus as a towering hero. In truth, the First Voyage did change history forever. Columbus had unwittingly doubled the known world. The greatest aftereffect centuries later was the United States as a new kind of democracy unknown in Europe.

By the five-hundredth anniversary of Columbus's first landfall, the United States was recognized as the most successful democracy ever. Its values included a growing interest in human rights. This caused scholars to look deeper into the dark side of Columbus. Historians pointed out that Columbus was the first European slaver in the Western Hemisphere. He set the tone and bore the responsibility for the destruction of millions of Indians. Las Casas supplied the Caribbean figures: one million on Hispaniola; 2 million in Paria.[18] The Spaniards destroyed the economies of major Indian empires, devastating the Inca realm so badly it has not recovered to this day. In addition, generations would suffer through five long centuries in the trail of the Spanish conquests. This included incalculable millions of American Indians and African slaves.

In 1509, King Ferdinand had given Ovando permission to raid the Bahamas to enslave the Lucayo.[19] Ferdinand later granted permission for two hundred fifty black slaves from West Africa to be shipped to the Indies to replace the shrinking Arawak population. Instead of converting the Indians of the Caribbean, Paria, and Lake Maracaibo, the Spaniards

Bartholomew de las Casas railed against the Spanish reign of terror on the Indians. His writings of such atrocities came to be called the "Black Legend."

had robbed them, enslaved them, and exterminated them. Spanish fleets raided the Venezuelan coast for years to load up with Indian slaves. A third died on the voyage to Spanish slave marts, probably from dehydration.

In 1528, Spain contracted the Indian slave trade to a powerful German banking house. They gave it rights to hunt and sell human cargo from the mainland Arawak.[20] Las Casas believed atrocities in Venezuela outpaced those in the Caribbean. Meanwhile, the black slave trade was in progress from Africa, coming into the Americas.

Today, five hundred years after the discovery of the Western Hemisphere, scholars are still engaged in the rediscovery of Columbus. It is for new readers in the modern era to decide Columbus's place in history, and to learn from the crimes against humanity that followed his first landfall.

Timeline

ca. 1451—Christopher Columbus is born in the northern Italian city-state of Genoa; The family speaks Spanish at home; Their origins are obscure.

ca. 1465 –1476—He sails the Mediterranean and to England (and perhaps Iceland) in the North Atlantic; He runs a map store in Lisbon.

1479—He marries into the nobility and becomes a traveling salesman in the lower North Atlantic.

1484—He presents his plan to cross the Sea of Darkness to King John II of Portugal; It is rejected.

1486—He presents the Enterprise of the Indies to Spanish king and queen Ferdinand and Isabella; Years later, it is turned down.

1492—Castile and Aragon conquer Granada; Columbus is recalled and signs a contract with Castile.

1492 –1493—Columbus's First Voyage: Columbus discovers the Bahamas, Cuba, and Haiti.

1493 —Columbus's Second Voyage: Columbus
–1496 discovers the Lesser and Greater Antilles chain of Caribbean islands and Jamaica; He founds the colony of Isabella in Haiti; He seizes Taíno men and women as slave cargo and sends them back to Spain; Ojeda wins smashing victories against poorly armed Haitian Indians; Columbus creates the gold tax; A gold mine is discovered in the south near Santo Domingo.

1498 —Columbus's Third Voyage: Columbus
–1500 discovers Trinidad, the Orinoco delta, and Paria; Columbus starts the plantation system in the Western Hemisphere; Da Gama sails to India and back; The three Columbus brothers are sent home in chains by Bobadilla.

1499 —Amerigo Vespucci, an Italian living in Spain, sails under command of Alonso de Ojeda; They explore the northern coast of South America.

1500 —Vicente Yañez Pinzón explores the northern coast of South America down to Brazil and discovers the mouth of the Amazon River; Vespucci claims he did it first.

1502 —Columbus's Fourth Voyage: Columbus
–1504 discovers Honduras, Nicaragua, Costa Rica, and Panama; He is shipwrecked for a year on Jamaica; King Ferdinand retires him.

1506 —Columbus dies in comfortable circumstances believing India lies just beyond Panama.

1509 —Ojeda leads expedition into northern Colombia, is wounded, and dies in Santo Domingo in great pain.

1515 —Two schools of thought arise about Columbus
–1550 and the conquistadors. One is founded by Las
Casas, and decries the excessive cruelty of the
Spaniards; The other, by Oviedo, sees
Columbus as a great hero for Spain.

1992 —After five hundred years, and in an era of
democracy in the West, there is a growing
disgust with the viciousness of the Spanish
conquests; Columbus is increasingly seen as
having character flaws that reflect back upon
the reign of terror of Inquisition Spain.

Chapter Notes

Chapter 1. A Strange Land

1. Miles H. Davidson, *Columbus Then and Now: A Life Reexamined* (Norman: University of Oklahoma Press, 1997), pp. 116–117.

2. John Fiske, *The Discovery of America*, 2 vols. (Boston: Houghton Mifflin, 1892), vol. 1, p. 353.

3. Washington Irving, *History of the Life and Voyages of Christopher Columbus*, 2 vols. (London: Murray, 1828), reprinted (New York: Putnam's, 3 vols. in 1), vol. 1, pp. 198–199.

4. Ibid, p. 185.

5. Paolo E. Taviani, *Columbus: The Great Adventure* (New York: Orion, 1991), p. 94.

6. Davidson, p. 218.

7. Samuel E. Morison, *Admiral of the Ocean Sea* (Boston: Little Brown, 1942), p. 221.

8. Ibid., p. 221.

9. Davidson, p. 223.

10. Ibid., p. 152.

11. Zvi Dor-Ner with William G. Scheller, *Columbus and the Age of Discovery* (New York: Morrow, 1991), p. 176.

12. R. H. Major, ed., *Christopher Columbus: Four Voyages to the New World, Letters and Selected Documents* (New York: Corinth Books, 1961), pp. 9–10.

13. Irving, p. 325.

Chapter 2. A Boy's Dreams

1. Miles H. Davidson, *Columbus Then and Now: A Life Reexamined* (Norman: University of Oklahoma Press, 1997), p. xxi.

2. Ibid.

3. Ibid., p. xxv.

4. Ibid., p. xxviii.

5. Ibid.

6. Zvi Dor-Ner with William G. Scheller, *Columbus and the Age of Discovery* (New York: Morrow, 1991), p. 45.

7. John Noble Wilford, *The Mysterious History of Columbus* (New York: Knopf, 1991), p. 61.

8. Paolo E. Taviani, *Columbus: The Great Adventure* (New York: Orion, 1991), p. 4.

9. Ibid., p. 12.

10. Ibid., p. 15.

11. Michael D. Lemonick and Andrea Dorfman, "The Amazing Vikings," *Time*, May 8, 2000, p. 74.

12. Taviani, pp. 53–54.

Chapter 3. What Was Then Known

1. Samuel E. Morison, *Admiral of the Ocean Sea* (Boston: Little Brown, 1942), p. 68.

2. Ibid.

3. Ibid.

4. Salvador de Madariaga, *Christopher Columbus, Being the Life of the Very Magnificent Lord Don Cristóbal Colón* (New York: Macmillan, 1940), p. 18.

5. Ibid.

6. Ibid., p. 431.

7. Paolo E. Taviani, *Columbus: The Great Adventure* (New York: Orion, 1991), pp. 31–32.

8. Daniel J. Boorstin, *The Discoverers: A History of Man's Search to Know His World and Himself* (New York: Random House, 1983), p. 168.

9. John Dyson, *Columbus: For Gold, God and Glory: In Search of the Real Christopher Columbus* (New York: Simon & Schuster, 1991), p. 54; Morison, p. 390.

10. Boorstin, pp. 169–170.

Chapter 4. Bending the Law

1. John Dyson, *Columbus: For Gold, God and Glory: In Search of the Real Christopher Columbus* (New York: Simon & Schuster, 1991), p. 69.

2. Ibid., p. 71.

3. Samuel E. Morison, *Admiral of the Ocean Sea* (Boston: Little Brown, 1942), pp. 73–74.

4. Ibid., pp. 75–76.

5. Washington Irving, *History of the Life and Voyages of Christopher Columbus*, 2 vols. (London: Murray, 1828), reprinted (New York: Putnam's, 3 vols. in 1), vol. 2, p. 18.

6. Zvi Dor-Ner with William G. Scheller, *Columbus and the Age of Discovery* (New York: Morrow, 1991), p. 104.

7. Salvador de Madariaga, *Christopher Columbus, Being the Life of the Very Magnificent Lord Don Cristóbal Colón* (New York: Macmillan, 1940), p. 119.

8. Ibid., p. 120.

9. B. Netanyahu, *The Origins of the Inquisition in Fifteenth Century Spain* (New York: Random House, 1995), pp. 1006–1007.

10. Ibid., p. 1087.

11. Kirkpatrick Sale, *The Conquest of Paradise: Christopher Columbus and the Columbian Legacy* (New York: Knopf, 1990), p. 16.

12. Dor-Ner with Scheller, p. 103.

13. Heinrich Graetz, *History of the Jews* (Philadelphia: Jewish Publication Society, 1894), 6 vols., vol. 4, pp. 355–356.

Chapter 5. Where in the World Was He?

1. Washington Irving, *History of the Life and Voyages of Christopher Columbus*, 2 vols. (London: Murray, 1828), reprinted (New York: Putnam's, 3 vols. in 1), vol. 1, p. 330.

2. Ibid., pp. 376–378.

3. Ibid., p. 392.

4. John Fiske, *The Discovery of America*, 2 vols. (Boston: Houghton Mifflin, 1892) vol. 1, pp. 460–461.

5. Samuel E. Morison, *Admiral of the Ocean Sea* (Boston: Little Brown, 1942), p. 397.

6. Fiske, pp. 460–461.

7. Irving, vol. 2, p. 28.

8. Morison, p. 416.

9. John Noble Wilford, *The Mysterious History of Columbus* (New York: Knopf, 1991), p. 178.

10. Irving, p. 382.

Chapter 6. People of the Americas

1. Andrea Dorfman, "New Ways to the New World," *Time*, April 17, 2000, p. 70.

2. Miguel Covarrubias, *The Eagle, the Jaguar, and the Serpent* (New York: Knopf, 1967), pp. 25–28.

3. Dorfman, p. 70.

4. Irving Rouse, *The Taínos: Rise and Decline of the People Who Greeted Columbus* (New Haven: Yale University Press, 1992), p. 5.

5. Ibid., p. 8.

6. Ibid., p. 7.

7. Kirkpatrick Sale, *The Conquest of Paradise: Christopher Columbus and the Columbian Legacy* (New York: Knopf, 1990), p. 160.

8. Rouse, p. 9.

9. Ibid., p. 12.

10. R. H. Major, ed., *Christopher Columbus: Four Voyages to the New World, Letters and Selected Documents* (New York: Corinth Books, 1961), pp. 29–31.

11. Ibid., p. 7.

12. Zvi Dor-Ner with William G. Scheller, *Columbus and the Age of Discovery* (New York: Morrow, 1991), p. 209.

13. Francine Jacobs, *The Taínos* (New York: Putnam's, 1992), p. 64.

Chapter 7. War With Caonabó

1. John Fiske, *The Discovery of America*, 2 vols. (Boston: Houghton Mifflin, 1892), vol. 1, p. 466.

2. Washington Irving, *History of the Life and Voyages of Christopher Columbus*, 2 vols. (London: Murray, 1828), reprinted (New York: Putnam's, 3 vols. in 1), vol. 1, p. 397.

3. Samuel E. Morison, *Admiral of the Ocean Sea* (Boston: Little Brown, 1942), p. 441.

4. John Noble Wilford, *The Mysterious History of Columbus* (New York: Knopf, 1991), p. 174.

5. Ibid., p. 172.

6. Kirkpatrick Sale, *The Conquest of Paradise: Christopher Columbus and the Columbian Legacy* (New York: Knopf, 1990), p. 149.

7. Ibid., p. 153.

8. Irving, vol. 2, p. 237.

9. Morison, pp. 431–432.

10. Ibid., pp. 442–443.

11. Fiske, p. 479.

12. Morison, p. 484.

13. Ibid., p. 489.

14. Irving, vol.2, pp. 238–239.

Chapter 8. No Fair Trial

1. Kirkpatrick Sale, *The Conquest of Paradise: Christopher Columbus and the Columbian Legacy* (New York: Knopf, 1990), p. 155.

2. Ibid.

3. Ibid., p. 160.

4. Bartolomé de las Casas, *A Short Account of the Destruction of the Indies* (London: Penguin, 1992), p. 92.

5. R. H. Major, ed., *Christopher Columbus: Four Voyages to the New World, Letters and Selected Documents* (New York: Corinth Books, 1961), pp. 120, 123, 124.

6. Francine Jacobs, *The Taíno* (New York: Putnam's, 1992), p. 77.

7. Daniel J. Boorstin, *The Discoverers: A History of Man's Search to Know His World and Himself* (New York: Random House, 1983), p. 177.

8. Vasco de Gama, "The Route to India, 1497–8," *Portuguese Voyages 1498–1663*, ed. Charles David Ley, (London: Dent, 1947), p. 28.

9. Ibid.

10. Las Casas, pp. 96–101.

11. Sale, p. 156.

Chapter 9. In Search of Columbus

1. Kirkpatrick Sale, *The Conquest of Paradise: Christopher Columbus and the Columbian Legacy* (New York: Knopf, 1990), p. 159.

2. John Noble Wilford, *The Mysterious History of Columbus* (New York: Knopf, 1991), p. 61.

3. Bartolomé de las Casas, *A Short Account of the Destruction of the Indies* (London: Penguin, 1992), p. xiii.

4. John Fiske, *The Discovery of America*, 2 vols. (Boston: Houghton Mifflin, 1892), vol. 2, p. 438.

5. Las Casas, p. xviii.

6. Ibid., p. 15; Sale, p. 157.

7. Las Casas, p. 22.

8. Sale, p. 218.

9. William H. Prescott, *History of the Conquest of Peru* (New York: Modern Library, 1998), p. 150.

10. Fiske, p. 162.

11. Felipe Fernández-Armesto, *Columbus* (New York: Oxford University Press, 1991), p. 187.

12. Ibid., p. 186.

13. Fiske, p. 152.

14. Samuel E. Morison, *Admiral of the Ocean Sea* (Boston: Little Brown, 1942), p. 666.

15. Sale, p. 223.

16. Las Casas, p. xiii.

17. Ibid., p. 341.

18. Las Casas, p. 92.

19. Francine Jacobs, *The Taínos* (New York: Putnam's, 1992), p. 79.

20. Las Casas, p. 96.

Further Reading

Dodge, Steven C. *Christopher Columbus and the First Voyage to the New World*. New York: Chelsea House Publishers, 1991.

Isaacs, Sally. *Columbus (Prehistory to 1585): From Earliest Times to 1585*. Heinemann Library, 1998.

Jones, Mary E., ed. *Christopher Columbus and His Legacy: Opposing Viewpoints*. Greenhaven Press, Inc., 1992.

Postgate, Oliver. *Columbus: The Triumphant Failure*. New York: Franklin Watts, Inc., 1992.

Scavone, Daniel C. *Christopher Columbus*. Lucent Books, 1992.

Stein, Conrad R. *Christopher Columbus*. Children's Press, 1992.

Szumski, Bonnie. *Christopher Columbus: Recognizing Stereotypes*. Greenhaven Press, Inc., 1992.

Internet Addresses

Halsall, Paul. "Medieval Sourcebook: Christopher Columbus: Extracts from Journal." *Fordham University*. <http://www.fordham.edu/halsall/source/columbus1.html>.

Library of Congress. January 2, 2001. *The Caribbean-Island Society*. <http://lcweb.loc.gov/exhibits/1492/>.

Pickering, Keith A. "Examining the History, Navigation, and Landfall of Christopher Columbus." *The Columbus Navigation Homepage*. (1997–2000) <http://www1.minn.net/~keithp/>.

Index